From Oracle Bone Inscriptions to the World of Chinese Language:

A Chinese-English Bilingual Edition of
150 Commonly Used Characters

从甲骨文走向汉语世界：

150个常见汉字中英文双语对照本

王本兴著　蒋文杰译

图书在版编目（CIP）数据

从甲骨文走向汉语世界：150个常见汉字中英文双语对照本/王本兴著；蒋文杰译. —福州：福建教育出版社，2025.7. —ISBN 978-7-5758-0230-7

Ⅰ.H195.4

中国国家版本馆CIP数据核字第20247CP590号

责任编辑：朱蕴茝
特约编辑：黄爱华
美术编辑：季凯闻

Cong Jiaguwen Zouxiang Hanyu Shijie：150 Ge Changjian Hanzi Zhongyingwen Shuangyu Duizhaoben

从甲骨文走向汉语世界：150个常见汉字中英文双语对照本

王本兴著　蒋文杰译

出版发行	福建教育出版社
	（福州市梦山路27号　邮编：350025　网址：www.fep.com.cn
	编辑部电话：0591-83726908
	发行部电话：0591-83721876　87115073　010-62024258）
出 版 人	江金辉
印　　刷	福州德安彩色印刷有限公司
	（福州市金山工业区浦上标准厂房B区42栋）
开　　本	787毫米×1092毫米　1/16
印　　张	20
字　　数	328千字
插　　页	2
版　　次	2025年7月第1版　2025年7月第1次印刷
书　　号	ISBN 978-7-5758-0230-7
定　　价	79.00元

如发现本书印装质量问题，请向本社出版科（电话：0591-83726019）调换。

前　言

　　甲骨文是三千四百多年前中国古代社会的通用文字，是中国发现最早、最成熟、最成系统的古文字，是今天使用的汉字的源头和中国传统文化的根基。你一定好奇，这些文字，为什么叫甲骨文？因为三千多年前，中国人的祖先将文字刻在龟壳和动物骨头上，用来记录当时的天文、地理、历史、社会、军事、战争、农牧、人事、疾病等。然而由于历史原因，在之后的两三千年里，这些刻在龟壳和动物骨头上的文字，被埋藏在土地下面。后世的人们，即便在农耕时挖出了它们，也不知道这些刻着文字的甲骨到底是什么东西，导致这些远古的文明被随意丢弃或者毁坏。直到一个普通村民的出现，开始改变了这些甲骨文的命运。

　　这个普通的村民是一个走街串巷的理发师，由于劳累和自身不洁，有一次竟然染上了一身脓疮。这个时候，日常照顾他生意的村民们怕被理发师身上的怪病给传染上，都躲得远远的。没有生意可做的理发师，穷得连治病的钱都没有。可怜的理发师在一次散步途中，发现了一些被丢到河边的甲骨，看着上面神奇的文字和图案，迷信的理发师觉得，或许这是上天赐给他的良药，于是他把这些甲骨收集起来，碾成粉末，涂在身上的脓疮上，想不到奇迹竟然出现了，疮面的脓水被这些骨粉给吸干了。这些骨粉，真的能止血吗？为了进一步试验，这名理发师用刀片划破自己的手，把骨粉敷到流血的伤口上，血居然又被止住了。

　　甲骨能止血的事，很快就传遍了小村子。村上一些老人觉得，甲骨能止血，是神仙在显灵，而读过一些书的人，则说这些甲骨就是龙的骨头，可以治百病。于是，理发师在他的脓疮治愈后，就不再干理发这一行了，而是去沟渠、田间、河滩等地方，把别人扔掉的龙骨（大多无文字刻画）收集起来，拿到中药铺去卖。起初药铺不知何物也不敢收，他就当场表演了止血的试验，药铺掌柜就以比较高的价格将这些甲骨收购。久而久之，"龙骨"开始走进了中药铺，当作"刀创药"，出售行市。其他的农民听说这些甲骨能卖钱，也开始收集起来。随着时间的推移，人们对甲骨的需求越来越大。很快这件事就传向四面八方，周围的农民也纷纷前来挖掘。

120多年前，北京有一个叫王懿荣的中国学者，他生了一个怪病，用了许多药，就是不见好转。当时北京的一位名医给他开了一剂药方，药方上一味龙骨中药吸引了他的目光。怎么还有药叫龙骨呢？于是他在北京买回了一些很小的龙骨。回家后，他翻看再三，摩挲良久，也没有看出什么名堂来，但是他觉得这些叫"龙骨"的中药一定不寻常。于是他便抱病亲临药房叮嘱药房老板，如果再有商贩送"龙骨"来，一定要告诉他。没过几天，真有人给他送来了12片"龙骨"。这些"龙骨"因为比较大，王懿荣在上面发现了许多刻画。在伏案查阅许多资料之后，王懿荣猜测这些甲骨上的刻画，应该是三千多年前老祖先留下来的古文字。

于是，王懿荣把北京各大药店里刻有文字的甲骨全部买下，后来又从另一个朋友那儿收购了数百片。最后王懿荣收购的甲骨有1500多片。王懿荣把一块块精心整理过的龟甲兽骨给许多社会名流品鉴观赏，并郑重地告诉大家：甲骨片上镌刻的"画纹符号"是文字，是中国最古老的文字！这一重大发现，中国文化界为之轰动，世界学术界为之震撼！也正因王懿荣对甲骨文的发现，他被誉为"甲骨文之父"！王懿荣之后，中国又出现了许多知名的甲骨文研究学者，他们为甲骨文的发展作出了巨大贡献。由于世界各国甲骨文学者的不断努力，目前甲骨文已出土了15万片之多，甲骨文的研究者和爱好者也遍布全世界。2017年10月，甲骨文被联合国列入了《世界记忆名录》。这是中国的骄傲，更是人类的骄傲。

我是本书著作者，名叫王本兴，是中国甲骨文学者，在甲骨文领域拥有一定的专业知识，已正式出版了80多部著作，其中有30多部是甲骨文的专著。我们将携手共同努力，从甲骨文走向汉语世界，使更多的海内外读者能够深入了解全人类共同的文化遗产，推动甲骨文化普及与传播。

甲骨文是全人类的骄傲，是世界文化的瑰宝，更是认识汉字文化之源的开始，是补充人类智慧的需要。当下有些学习汉字的外国朋友，认为汉字难懂，不好学，所以很容易放弃。更重要的是，他们学了多年汉字与汉语，最后依然不会写，不会读，从而渐渐地丧失了继续学习中文的兴趣和信心。

基于这一点，由诸多国外汉语教学人士，通过多年教学经验及数据分析，筛选出"高频率"汉字150个，这就是本书《从甲骨文走向汉字世界：150个常见汉字中英文双语对照本》的由来。把这150个汉字与甲骨文字相应配合，从这150个甲骨文字开始，快速帮助国内外朋友阅读和书写，有效地走进汉语世界，重拾学习中文的信心。

《从甲骨文走向汉语世界：150个常见汉字中英文双语对照本》中的150个常用甲骨文字，每个字有示意图文，楷体标注，拼音识读，每个字有字源、出处、释义、引申义、常用组词、汉字的书写顺序等。每字附有两件甲骨文原始拓片，一字两页。本书所列甲骨文字，形、音、义皆备，简明扼要，易懂易记易识，学会、学好了这些常用甲骨文字，你会"登堂入室"，不断求索，终生受用。

学甲骨文并不难，事实证明，今天壮美、成熟的中国汉字，正是三千多年前孕育，然后诞生在中国殷商时代的"婴儿"，所以，从辈分上看，甲骨文字是中国汉字的"儿童文字"。亲爱的朋友，你一定会喜欢甲骨文，一定会学好甲骨文，一定能泰然自若地走进汉语世界，加油！

王本兴
中国南京鼓楼区凤凰西街59号四喜堂

Introduction

Oracle Bone Inscriptions (甲骨文 Jiǎ gǔ wén) is a universal script that emerged more than 3,400 years ago in ancient China. It represents the earliest, most mature, and systematic form of ancient Chinese writing, serving as the foundation for today's Chinese characters and traditional Chinese culture. You may wonder why it is called Oracle Bone Inscriptions. Over three millennia ago, Chinese ancestors engraved characters on turtle shells and animal bones to record astronomical, geographical, historical, social, military, war, farming, herding, personnel, and medical information. Due to historical circumstances, these inscriptions on turtle shells and animal bones were buried underground for the next two to three thousand years. Even when discovered during agricultural activities, people could not recognize these ancient civilizations, leading to their casual disposal or destruction.

Until an ordinary villager's finding, the fate of those Oracle Bone Inscriptions began to change.

This ordinary villager was a barber who wandered on the streets. His physical fatigue and lack of hygienic care caused him to develop infected with abscesses. At that time, the other villagers who used to visit him for haircuts were afraid of being infected by the strange disease on his body and kept their distance from him. With no business to do and lacking money for treatment, the unfortunate barber, during a stroll, stumbled upon some Oracle Bones discarded by the riverside. Observing the mysterious characters and patterns on them, the superstitious barber thought that perhaps was a divine medicine bestowed upon him. He collected these Oracle Bones, ground them into powder, and applied the powder to the infected wounds on his body. To his surprise, the bone powder absorbed the pus, effectively healing the sores. Could these bone fragments really stanch bleeding?

To further test this, the barber cut his own hand with a blade, applied the bone powder again to the bleeding wound, and astonishingly, the bleeding stopped.

The miraculous efficacy of Oracle Bones to stop bleeding quickly spread throughout the small village. Some elderly villagers believed it was the work of immortals, while those who had read some books claimed that these bones were dragon bones, capable of curing various ailments. After the barber's abscesses healed, he abandoned his career as a barber and started collecting discarded dragon bones (mostly without inscriptions) from ditches, fields, riverbanks, and other places. He sold these bones to traditional Chinese medicine shops. Initially, the shops were hesitant to purchase the bones, but the barber demonstrated the bleeding-stopping experiment in front of them. The shopkeepers then bought these Oracle Bones at a relatively high price. Over time, "dragon bones" made their way into traditional Chinese medicine shops, marketed as "wound-healing medicine". Other farmers, hearing that these Oracle Bones could be sold for money, also began collecting them. As demand for Oracle Bones increased, people from all around began excavating them.

More than 120 years ago, there was a Chinese scholar named Wang Yirong in Beijing who suffered from a peculiar illness. Despite trying many medicines, his condition did not improve. A local doctor in Beijing prescribed a medicine, and one of the ingredients on the prescription caught Wang Yirong's attention—dragon bones. Intrigued by the name, he purchased some small dragon bones in Beijing. Upon inspecting them at home, he couldn't make sense of the inscriptions despite repeated examinations and rubbings. However, he sensed that these so-called dragon bone medicines were extraordinary. Bearing his illness, Wang Yirong visited the pharmacy and instructed the owner to inform him if anyone brought more "dragon bones." In a few days, someone indeed delivered 12 pieces of "dragon bones" to him. Since these bones were relatively large, Wang Yirong discovered numerous engravings on them. After researching a wealth of materials, Wang Yirong speculated that the characters on these Oracle Bones were ancient writings left by our ancestors over three thousand years ago.

Subsequently, Wang Yirong purchased all the inscribed Oracle Bones from major drugstores in Beijing and acquired several hundred more pieces from another friend. In the end, Wang Yirong accumulated more than 1,500 pieces of Oracle Bones. He carefully organized these inscribed turtle shells and animal bones and showcased them to various social elites. He solemnly announced to everyone that the "pictographic symbols" engraved on Oracle Bone pieces were a form of writing, the oldest in China! This groundbreaking discovery sent shockwaves through the Chinese cultural community and resonated in the global academic sphere. Due to Wang Yirong's contribution to Oracle Bone Inscriptions, he earned the title of "Father of Oracle Bone Inscriptions". Following Wang Yirong, many renowned scholars in China emerged, making significant contributions to the development of Oracle Bone Inscriptions. Thanks to the continuous efforts of Oracle Bone scholars worldwide, around 150,000 pieces of Oracle Bones have been excavated. Researchers and enthusiasts of Oracle Bone Inscriptions are also found all over the world. Recognizing its cultural significance, the United Nations included Oracle Bone Inscriptions in the "Memory of the World Register" in October 2017. This is not only China's pride but also humanity's pride.

I am the author of this book, Wang Benxing, a Chinese Oracle Bone scholar with substantial expertise in the field. I have officially published over 80 works, including more than 30 focused on Oracle Bone Inscriptions. Together, let us strive to bridge the gap from Oracle Bone Inscriptions to the Chinese language world, enabling more readers worldwide to deeply understand our shared cultural heritage and promoting the dissemination of Oracle Bone culture.

Oracle Bone Inscriptions are the pride of all humanity, a treasure of world culture, and the starting point for understanding the origin of Chinese characters. Some foreign friends who learn Chinese characters today find them difficult to understand and challenging which makes them discouraged easily. More importantly, after years of studying Chinese characters and the language, they still struggle to read and write, gradually losing interest and confidence in continuing their Chinese language studies. Based on this, many foreign Chinese language educators, through years of teaching experience and data analysis, have selected

150 "high-frequency" Chinese characters. These characters are correspondingly matched with Oracle Bone characters. Starting with these 150 Oracle Bone characters will enable to help domestic and international friends read and write quickly, effectively immersing themselves in the Chinese language world and regaining confidence in learning Chinese.

The book "From Oracle Bone Inscriptions to the World of Chinese Language: A Chinese-English Bilingual Edition of 150 Commonly Used Characters" introduces 150 commonly used Oracle Bone characters. Each character is accompanied by illustrative images, standard script annotations, phonetic readings, origins, meanings, extended meanings, common word combinations, and the stroke order for writing the character. Each character is also accompanied by two original Oracle Bone Inscription rubbings and a page number. The listed Oracle Bone characters are comprehensive in form, sound, and meaning, concise and easy to understand, remember, and recognize. Mastering these commonly used Oracle Bone characters will allow you to "enter the door" and continue seeking knowledge, benefiting you throughout your life.

Learning Oracle Bone Inscriptions is not difficult. It has been proved that today's magnificent and mature Chinese characters were nurtured over three thousand years ago, giving birth to the "infant" during the Yin and Shang dynasties in China. Thus, in terms of generations, Oracle Bone Inscriptions are the "childhood characters" of Chinese characters. Dear friends, you will undoubtedly enjoy learning Oracle Bone Inscriptions, become proficient in them, and confidently enter the Chinese language world. Keep up the good work!

Wang Benxing
Sixi House, 59 Fenghuang West Street, Gulou District, Nanjing, China

目 录 Contents

第一单元 Unit 1 (2~21)

人、大、中、国、好
口、王、天、女、子

第二单元 Unit 2 (22~41)

我、日、小、力、男
在、不、土、家、门

第三单元 Unit 3 (42~61)

儿、看、学、酒、文
书、生、和、有、没

第四单元 Unit 4 (62~81)

月、明、朋、友、上
下、早、午、去、要

第五单元 Unit 5 (82~101)

一、二、三、四、五
六、七、八、九、十

第六单元 Unit 6 (102~121)

美、乐、山、易、老
师、可、以、长、者

第七单元 Unit 7 (122~141)

从、事、时、江、河
分、年、今、图、馆

第八单元 Unit 8 (142~161)

了、过、回、来、会
前、后、说、因、为

第九单元 Unit 9 (162~181)

出、面、自、己、同
心、两、得、就、能

第十单元 Unit 10 (182~201)

还、立、只、校、喜
京、习、听、东、西

第十一单元 Unit 11 (202~221)

南、北、比、如、最
高、名、复、旦、多

第十二单元 Unit 12 (222~241)

对、方、左、右、它、
知、道、用、林、森

第十三单元 Unit 13 (242~261)

身、起、成、次、进
作、第、发、行、正

第十四单元 Unit 14 (262~281)

世、亲、然、而、使
无、其、此、之、于

第十五单元 Unit 15 (282~301)

幸、福、望、由、安
木、水、火、阴、阳

后记 302

Afterword 304

第一单元

rén

人

甲骨文"人"字,像站立的人形,上端表示头,斜向伸展的表示手臂,中间部位是身子,最下部分表示腿脚。属象形字。

The Oracle Bone Script character "人" belongs to the category of pictograms. It depicts the side view of a standing person. The upper part represents the head. The diagonally extending lines symbolize the arms. The middle section represents the torso, and the lower part represents the legs and feet.

人(示意图)

第一单元

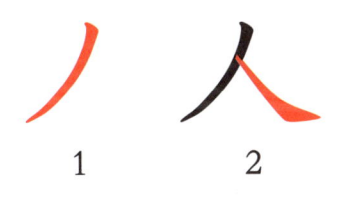

丿 人
1　2

楷书书写顺序

本义指人。引申为人类、成年人、民众、人才、人体、人道等义。

The original meaning of the character "人" refers to a person. It is extended to signify humanity, adults, the general public, talents, the human body, and the humane way, among other meanings.

人（甲骨文拓片）

与人组合的词有：人民、人生、人体、人山人海等。
Compound words related to the character "人" include:
1. 人民（rén mín）– People
2. 人生（rén shēng）– Life
3. 人体（rén tǐ）– Human body
4. 人山人海（rén shān rén hǎi）– Huge crowds

第一单元

dà
大

甲骨文"大"字,像一个正立的成人形,借成人的形象,又借人张开双手后的本身形状来表示超过一般或超过所比较的对象的意思。属象形字。

The Oracle Bone Script character "大" is categorized as a pictogram. It resembles the upright form of an adult, borrowing the image of an adult and further incorporating the shape formed when a person spreads his arms to convey the meaning of "big" and "large."

大(示意图)

第一单元

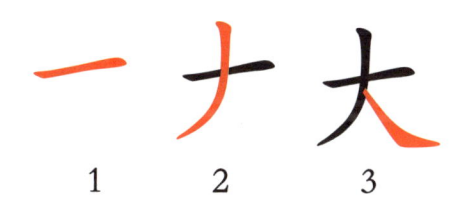

一 丿 大
1　2　3

楷书书写顺序

　　本义是指超过一般或超过所比较的对象（与"小"相对）。后引申为程度深、敬辞、专称、年长、排行第一、注重等义。

　　The original meaning of the character "大" is in opposition to "小," representing "big" or "large". Later, it extended to signify concepts such as depth, respect, formality, seniority, being the first in rank, emphasis, surpassing, and other related meanings.

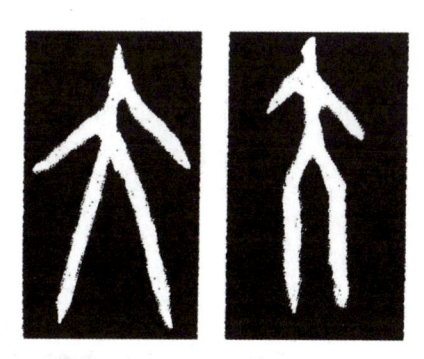

大（甲骨文拓片）

　　与大组合的词有：大学、大家、大会、大约等。
Compound words related to the character "大" include:
1. 大学（dà xué）– University
2. 大家（dà jiā）– Everyone; Great person
3. 大会（dà huì）– Grand assembly; Conference
4. 大约（dà yuē）– Approximately; About

第一单元

zhōng
中

甲骨文"中"字，像一面直立的旗帜，中竖为旗杆，上下有两条、四条不等的旗游，中部口字表示中间之意。有认为中间口字部表示所驻扎军营或氏族中心，以飘扬之旗帜为标志。另古时有大事，望"中"而趋赴，建"中"之地即为中央之中。属象形字。

The Oracle Bone Script character "中" is classified as a pictogram. It resembles an upright flag, where the vertical line represents the flagpole, and there are two to four fluttering flag lines above and below. The character "口" in the middle indicates the concept of the center. Some interpretations suggest that the central "口" character might represent a military camp or the center of a clan, symbolized by a flying flag. In ancient times, when significant events occurred, people would gather and move towards the direction of "中", establishing a place marked by "中" as the central location.

中（示意图）

第一单元

丨 冂 口 中
1　2　3　4

楷书书写顺序

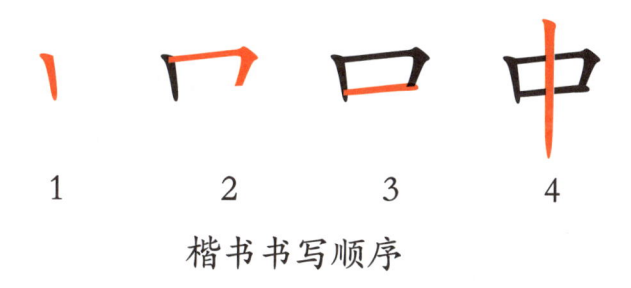

本义是旗帜。引申为中间、不偏不倚、等级在中间的、合适、成、中国等义。

The original meaning of the character "中" is a flag or banner. It is extended to convey meanings such as middle, impartial, being in the middle of a hierarchy, appropriate, accomplished, and China.

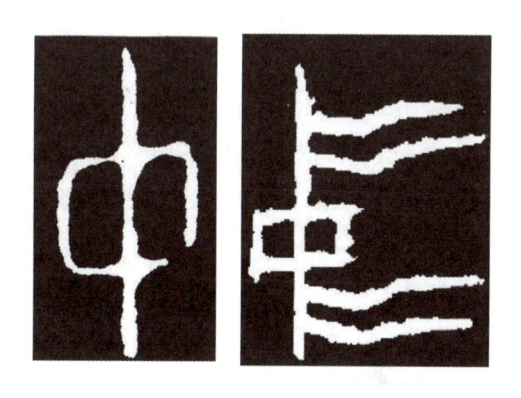

中（甲骨文拓片）

与中组合的词有：中国、中午、中学、中东、中秋等。

Compound words related to the character "中" include:

1. 中国（zhōng guó）– China
2. 中午（zhōng wǔ）– Noon; Midday
3. 中学（zhōng xué）– Middle school; Secondary school
4. 中东（zhōng dōng）– Middle East
5. 中秋（zhōng qiū）– Mid-Autumn

第一单元

guó

国

　　甲骨文"国"字是一个复合的表意文字,从口,从戈,口表示城池或国土,戈表示用武器守卫国土与城池。后口字部下端加一,表示范围界线。古邦国是一座城池及周边地域。作"或"字,后加土作"域",为地域之义。周围再加口(围)作"國",今汉字简化规范写作"国"为正体。属会意字。

　　The Oracle Bone Script character "国" is a compound ideogram consisting of the elements "口" (mouth) and "戈" (spear). The "口" represents a city or territory, and the "戈" signifies the use of weapons to defend the land and city. Later, the lower part of the "口" is extended with a horizontal line, symbolizing the boundary or territory. In ancient times, a state or nation was represented by a city and its surrounding areas. The character also functioned as a disjunctive, and when combined with "土" (earth/soil), it represented the concept of a territory. The addition of a surrounding "口" (enclosure) formed the character "國", which has been simplified to "国" in modern Chinese. Overall, "国" is a compound ideogram conveying the idea of a state or nation, and it falls under the category of ideographic characters.

国(示意图)

第一单元

丨	冂	冂	冂	同	国	国	国
1	2	3	4	5	6	7	8

楷书书写顺序

本义是邦国。可引申为都城、在一国内最出色的、代表属于本国的事物、姓等义。

The original meaning of the character "国" is a state or nation, specifically referring to a political entity. It can be extended to convey meanings such as the capital city, the most outstanding within a country, representing things belonging to one's own country, and family name (surname).

国（甲骨文拓片）

与国组合的词有：国家、国际、国防、国境等。
Compound words related to the character "国" include:
1. 国家（guó jiā）– Country; Nation
2. 国际（guó jì）– International
3. 国防（guó fáng）– National defense
4. 国境（guó jìng）– National border

第一单元

hǎo

好

其他读音：hào

甲骨文"好"字，从女，从子，右边像一个半跪着的女子，抱着一个婴儿，也可视为婴儿靠着女子。两形会意即指美好。上古时代女子能生儿育女，使氏族兴旺乃为美好。属象形会意字。

The Oracle Bone Script character "好" is a compound ideogram, combining the elements for "女"(woman) and "子"(child). On the right side, it resembles a woman in a half-kneeling position, holding an infant, or it can be interpreted as the infant leaning against the woman. The combination of these two elements signifies beauty or goodness. In ancient times, a woman's ability to give birth and raise children was seen as a symbol of prosperity for the clan, hence considered a manifestation of goodness or beauty.

好（示意图）

第一单元

く　 夂　 女　 女ˇ　 好　 好
1　 2　 3　 4　 5　 6

楷书书写顺序

本义是指母亲与孩子亲密美好之意。泛指美貌、美好。引申为与"坏"相对、善良、完美、完成、友爱、友好、完毕、可以、程度深数量多、答应等义。也指喜爱（与"恶"wù 相对）、容易，读 hào。

The original meaning of the character "好" refers to the intimate and beautiful relationship between a mother and her child. It has a broader sense, signifying beauty or goodness. It is extended to convey the opposite of "坏"（bad）, indicating kindness; it also represents perfection, completion, friendship, completion, ease, possibility, depth, abundance, agreement, and various other meanings.

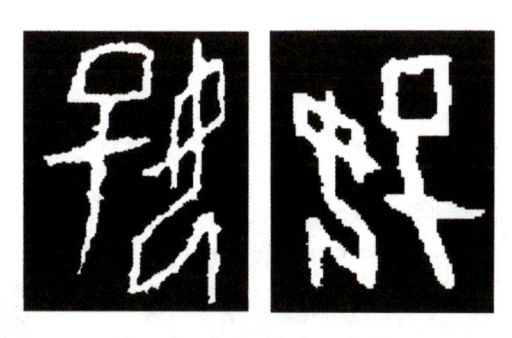

好（甲骨文拓片）

与好组合的词有：好事、好看、好笑、好奇心、好朋友等。
Compound words related to the character "好" include:
1. 好事（hǎo shì）– Good thing
2. 好看（hǎo kàn）– Good-looking
3. 好笑（hǎo xiào）– Funny
4. 好奇心（hào qí xīn）– Curiosity
5. 好朋友（hǎo péng yǒu）– Good friend

第一单元

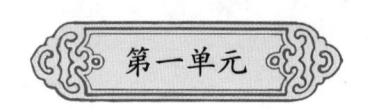

kǒu

口

甲骨文"口"字,像人张着口之形,口之功能有言、食。属象形字。

The Oracle Bone Script character "口" is a pictogram, representing the shape of an open mouth. The functions of the mouth include speech and eating.

口(示意图)

第一单元

1　2　3

楷书书写顺序

本义指人的嘴巴。可引申为言语、容器外口、破裂处、驴马年龄、人数、进出口、锋刃、行业与量词等义。

The original meaning of the character "口" refers to the mouth of a person and can be extended to signify: speech or spoken language, opening or mouth of a container, a place where something is cracked or broken, age of a donkey or horse, number of people, entrance and exit, sharp edge or blade, and industry and measure words.

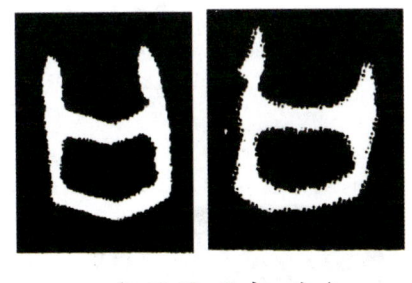

口（甲骨文拓片）

与口组合的词有：口袋、口腔、口水、口渴等。

Compound words related to the character "口" include:

1. 口袋（kǒu dài）– Pocket
2. 口腔（kǒu qiāng）– Oral cavity; Mouth
3. 口水（kǒu shuǐ）– Saliva
4. 口渴（kǒu kě）– Thirsty

第一单元

wáng

王

甲骨文"王"字，形如斧钺形，刃部向下。以斧钺主刑生杀大权象征王者权威。后于上部追加一横笔为饰画。属象形字。

The Oracle Bone Script character "王" takes on the shape of an axe or battle-ax, with the blade part pointing downward. This configuration symbolizes the authority of the king in wielding the power of life and death, serving as a representation of royal authority. Subsequently, an additional horizontal stroke was added to the upper part for decorative purposes. This character falls under the category of pictographic characters.

王（示意图）

第一单元

一 二 干 王
1　2　3　4

楷书书写顺序

本义是指大斧。可引申为最高统治者、首领、老辈尊称、称王、姓等义。后至秦代"皇"替代"王"，王遂成封爵之最高等级。

In Oracle Bone Script, the character "王" originally referred to a large axe. It can be extended to mean the highest ruler, leader, and is also used as an honorific for elders. It can denote a king or be used as a surname. Later, during the Qin Dynasty, the term "皇" replaced "王" as the title for an emperor, and "王" became the highest title for nobility.

王（甲骨文拓片）

与王组合的词有：王牌、王国、王子等。
Compound words related to the character "王" include:
1. 王牌（wáng pái）– Ace（playing card）; Top player or performer
2. 王国（wáng guó）– Kingdom
3. 王子（wáng zǐ）– Prince

第一单元

tiān

天

甲骨文"天"字，下从大，像正面人形，上从O、口，像人之头顶，或从二，或从一，皆指头顶蓝天之意。属象形字。

The Oracle Bone Script character "天" belongs to the category of pictograms. The lower part consists of the " 大 " character, symbolizing the front view of a person. The upper part includes the shape of "O" or "口", representing the top of a person's head. Sometimes, it is represented by the shapes "二" or "一", all indicating the concept of the sky above the head. This character signifies the vast space above the head, representing the blue sky.

天（示意图）

第一单元

一 二 于 天
1　　2　　3　　4
楷书书写顺序

本义是指头顶。可引申为位在上的、天空、天气、自然、某一空间等义。

The original meaning is "overhead". It can be extended to mean located above, sky, weather, nature, a certain space, etc.

天（甲骨文拓片）

与天组合的词有：天地、天文、天空等。
Compound words related to the charater "天" include:
1. 天地（tiān dì）– Heaven and Earth
2. 天文（tiān wén）– Astronomy
3. 天空（tiān kōng）– Sky

第一单元

nǚ
女

甲骨文"女"字，像是一女子屈膝交手跪坐之形。属象形字。

In Oracle Bone Script, the character "女" depicts the form of a woman kneeling with bent knees and clasped hands. It belongs to the category of pictograms.

女（示意图）

第一单元

く 夊 女
1　2　3

楷书书写顺序

本义是指未出嫁的女子。可引申为女性的、女儿、幼小、幼名等义。

The original meaning refers to an unmarried woman. It can be extended to mean female, daughter, young, childhood name, etc.

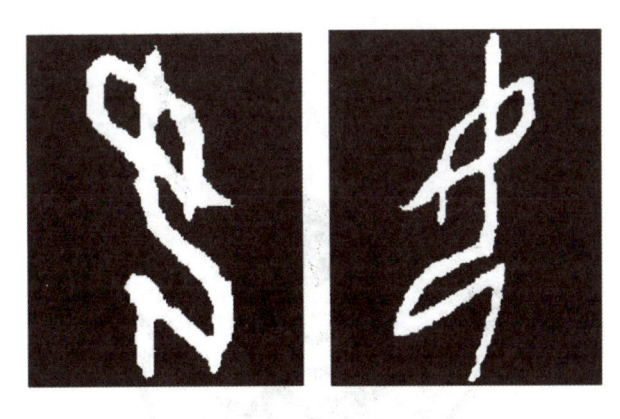

女（甲骨文拓片）

与女组合的词有：女儿、女孩、女皇、女朋友等。

Compound words related to character "女" include:

1. 女儿（nǚ ér）- Daughter
2. 女孩（nǚ hái）- Girl
3. 女皇（nǚ huáng）- Empress
4. 女朋友（nǚ péng you）- Girlfriend

第一单元

zǐ

子

甲骨文"子"字,像是有头发、囟门和身子的新生儿形。并像在襁褓之中,有的子字头上有发,两臂舞动,两腿裹在被子中,故身躯可写成一竖。属象形字。

In Oracle Bone Script, the character "子" depicts the form of a newborn with head, fontanelle, and body. It resembles an infant in swaddling clothes, with some versions showing hair on the head, arms waving, and legs wrapped in a blanket, allowing the body to be represented as a vertical line. This character belongs to the category of pictograms.

子(示意图)

第一单元

了 子
1　2　3

楷书书写顺序

本义是指婴儿。可引申为儿女、人、对男子的尊称、有德行的老师、诸子百家著作、封爵的第四等义。借用作地支第一位，用以纪时、纪日、纪年。"子时"即夜里十一时至次日凌晨一时。

The original meaning refers to an infant. It can be extended to mean children, people, an honorable title for a man, a teacher of virtue, works of various schools of thought, and the fourth rank of nobility. Used as the first Earthly Branch in the Chinese zodiac to mark hours, days, and years. "子时" refers to the period from eleven o'clock at night to one o'clock in the early morning of the next day.

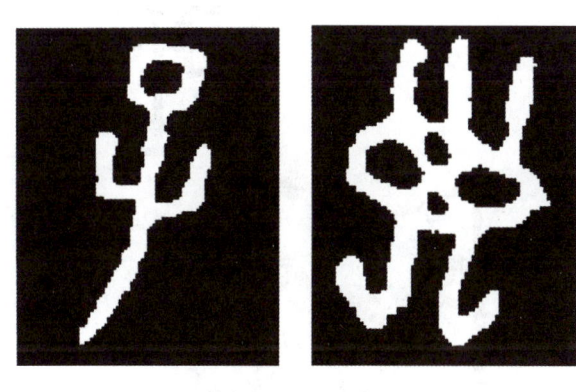

子（甲骨文拓片）

与子组合的词有：子女、子弹、子弟、子孙后代等。
Compound words related to the character "子" include:
1. 子女（zǐ nǚ）– Sons and daughters; Children
2. 子弹（zǐ dàn）– Bullet
3. 子弟（zǐ dì）– Younger generation; Younger brothers
4. 子孙后代（zǐ sūn hòu dài）– Descendants; Posterity

第二单元

wǒ

我

甲骨文"我"字,像是带牙齿的刀锯之形,或作带有长柄的三锋之戈,或作屠宰牲畜用具。属象形字。

The Oracle Bone Script character "我" is depicted as a form resembling a saw or knife with teeth. Sometimes it is represented as a three-edged dagger with a long handle or a tool used for slaughtering animals. This character belongs to the category of pictograms.

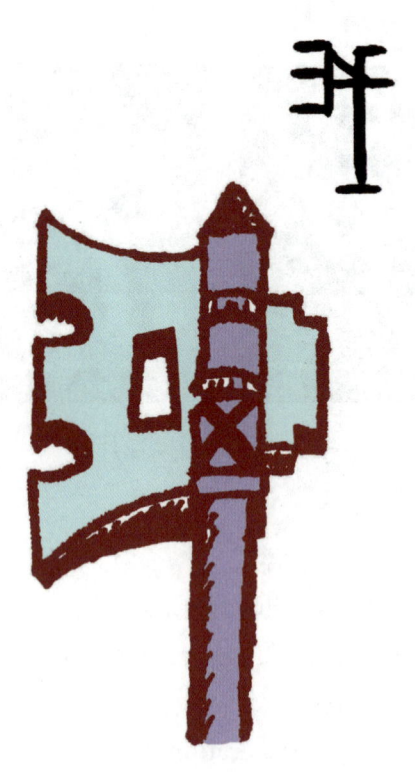

我(示意图)

第二单元

丿 二 千 手 扚 我 我
1　2　3　4　5　6　7

楷书书写顺序

　　本义是指锯齿状兵器。后本义废，引申为第一人称我、自己、刀锯类工具、刑具等义。

The original meaning refers to a serrated weapon. Over time, this original meaning was abandoned, and it is extended to mean the first-person pronoun "我"（I/me）, oneself, tools resembling saws, and instruments of punishment.

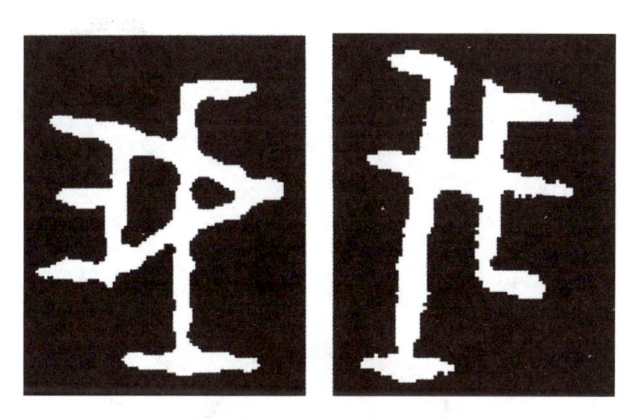

我（甲骨文拓片）

　　与我组合的词有：我们、我国、我行我素等。
Compound words related to the character "我" include:
1. 我们（wǒ men）– We; Us
2. 我国（wǒ guó）– Our country
3. 我行我素（wǒ xíng wǒ sù）– Stick to one's own way

rì

日

甲骨文"日"字,像太阳之形。甲骨文中的日字都是圆圈中加一个小黑点,那是因为可以有别于口字。后来为了便于用刀刻写甲骨文,日的轮廓方形间改作一横。属象形字。

The Oracle Bone Script character "日" is a pictogram, resembling the shape of the sun. In oracle bone script, the character for "日" is represented by a circle with a small black dot, distinguishing it from the character for "口"(mouth). Later, for ease of inscription using a knife in oracle bone script, the contour of "日" was modified to include a horizontal line within a square.

日(示意图)

第二单元

丨 冂 冃 日
1　2　3　4

楷书书写顺序

本义是太阳。引申为白天、每天、时间、吉凶、禁忌、时辰等义。

The original meaning of "日" refers to the sun. It is extended to mean daytime, every day, time, auspicious or inauspicious events, taboos, and specific time periods.

日（甲骨文拓片）

与日组合的词有：日程、日出、日落、日期、日常、日记、日新月异等。
Compound words related to the character "日" include:

1. 日程（rì chéng）– Schedule
2. 日出（rì chū）– Sunrise
3. 日落（rì luò）– Sunset
4. 日期（rì qī）– Date
5. 日常（rì cháng）– Daily
6. 日记（rì jì）– Diary
7. 日新月异（rì xīn yuè yì）– Constantly changing and improving

第二单元

xiǎo

小

甲骨文"小"字，从三点或三短画，指"物之微也"，但不知"微"是指什么事物。大概是用沙粒表示微小之具象，会微小之意。属象形会意字。

The Oracle Bone Script character "小" is a combination of pictorial and ideographic elements, consisting of three dots or short strokes, representing the concept of "minuteness" in objects. However, it is unclear what specific object is referred to by "minuteness". Perhaps the use of grains of sand is employed to symbolize the concrete idea of smallness.

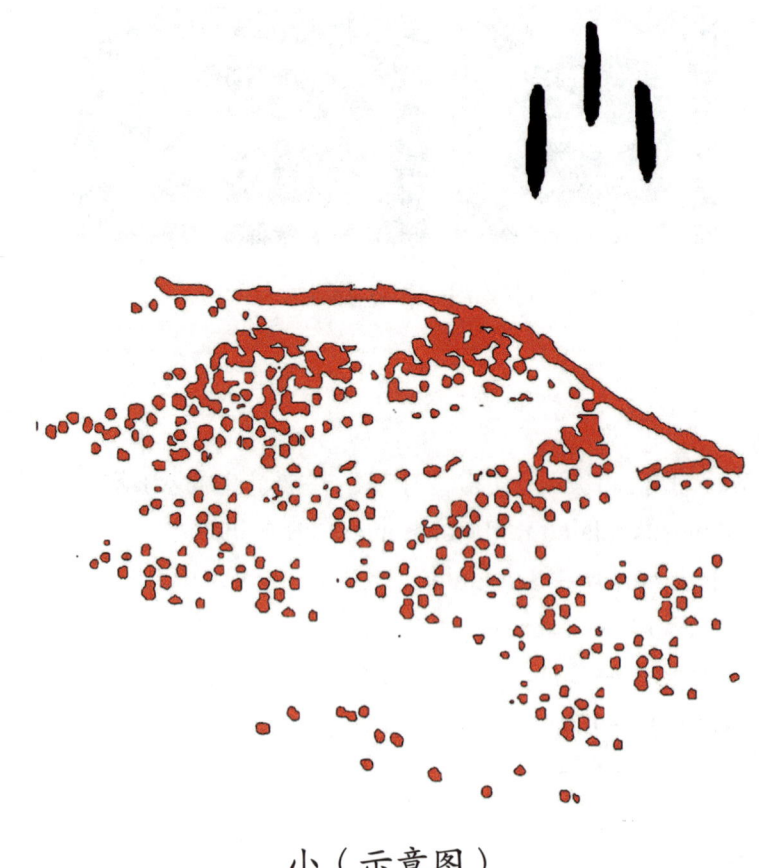

小（示意图）

第二单元

亅 小 小
1　2　3

楷书书写顺序

本义与"大"相反，指细小。引申为面积小、地方小、数量少、时间短、声音低、稍微、低微、自谦等义。

The original meaning of "小" is opposite to "大"（big）, referring to something small or fine. It is extended to mean small in area, limited in space, few in quantity, short in time, low in volume, a bit, slight, humble, and other related meanings.

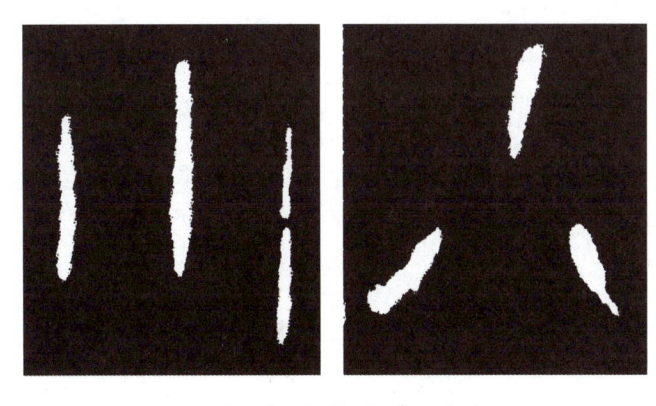

小（甲骨文拓片）

与小组合的词有：小学、小镇、小雨、小孩、小麦、小提琴等。

Compound words related to the character "小" include:

1. 小学（xiǎo xué）– Primary school
2. 小镇（xiǎo zhèn）– Small town
3. 小雨（xiǎo yǔ）– Light rain
4. 小孩（xiǎo hái）– Child
5. 小麦（xiǎo mài）– Wheat
6. 小提琴（xiǎo tí qín）– Violin

第二单元

力

甲骨文"力"字,像犁地所用的耒形。在耕田时须用力,用耒时也用力,所以先人造字时用耒形来表示"力"。属象形字。

The Oracle Bone Script character "力" resembles the shape of the plowshare used for plowing the land. Since exerting force is necessary when plowing the fields and using the plow, the concept of "力"（strength or force）was represented by the character for plowshare in ancient times. This character belongs to the category of pictograms.

力（示意图）

第二单元

力

1　2

楷书书写顺序

　　本义是指耒。后引申为力气、体力、力量、能力、权力、权势、劳动、劳作、功劳、尽力而为等义。

The original meaning refers to plowshare. It is extended to mean physical strength, power, capability, authority, labor, work, merit, and the concept of doing one's utmost.

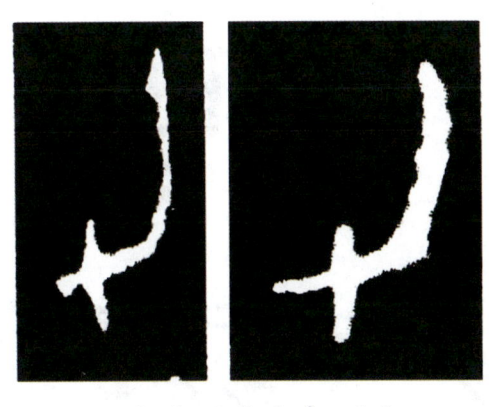

力（甲骨文拓片）

　　与力组合的词有：力量、力度、力所能及等。

Compound words related to the character "力" include:

1. 力量（lì liàng）– Strength; Power
2. 力度（lì dù）– Intensity
3. 力所能及（lì suǒ néng jí）– Within one's capacity

nán

男

甲骨文"男"字，从田，从耒（犁），此借以耒耕田可会男子之意，因男子主事农耕。属会意字。

The Oracle Bone Script character "男" is composed of the radical "田"(field) and "耒"(plow, represented by the plowshare). It was borrowed to convey the idea of men engaged in plowing fields, as men were primarily responsible for agricultural activities. This character belongs to the category of ideograms indicating a combined concept.

男（示意图）

第二单元

丿 冂 冂 日 田 田 男

1　2　3　4　5　6　7

楷书书写顺序

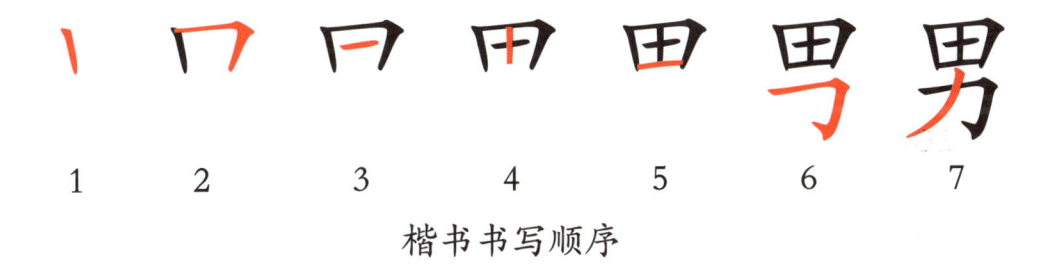

本义是指男子。可引申为儿子、爵位第五、男儿等义。

The original meaning refers to man. It can be extended to mean son, the fifth rank of nobility, and young man, among other related concepts.

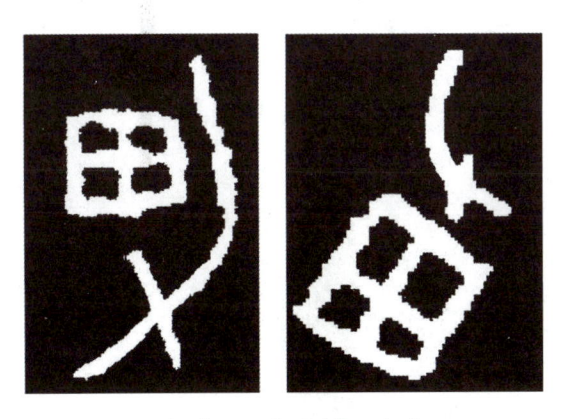

男（甲骨文拓片）

与男组合的词有：男孩、男装、男朋友、男子汉、男女平等等。

Compound words related to the character "男" include:

1. 男孩（nán hái）– Boy
2. 男装（nán zhuāng）– Men's clothing
3. 男朋友（nán péng yǒu）– Boyfriend
4. 男子汉（nán zǐ hàn）– Real man; Manly man
5. 男女平等（nán nǚ píng děng）– Gender equality

31

zài

在

甲骨文"在"字,通"才",像草木初萌,拔地而出的样子,表示植物破土而生成。属象形字。

The Oracle Bone Script character "在", also written as "才", depicts the appearance of plants sprouting and emerging from the ground, symbolizing the growth of vegetation. This character belongs to the category of pictograms.

在(示意图)

第二单元

一 ナ 才 存 存 在
1　2　3　4　5　6
楷书书写顺序

本义是指草木初生。后引申为存在、留在、正在、动作进行等义。

The original meaning of the character "在" refers to the initial growth of plants. It is extended to mean existence, staying, being in the process of, and ongoing actions, etc.

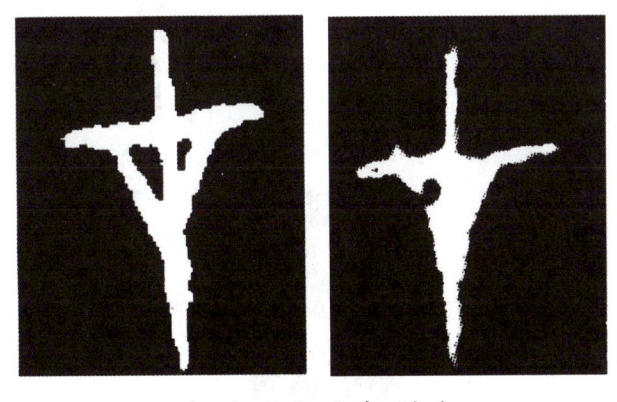

在（甲骨文拓片）

与在组合的词有：在位、在外、在家、在场、在此之前等。
Compound words related to the character "在" include:
1. 在位（zài wèi）– In office; In position
2. 在外（zài wài）– Outside
3. 在家（zài jiā）– At home
4. 在场（zài chǎng）– Present; On the scene
5. 在此之前（zài cǐ zhī qián）– Before this; Prior to this

第二单元

bù

不

甲骨文"不"字,像花倒着的花萼形状。属象形字。

The Oracle Bone Script character "不" is a pictographic character that resembles the inverted shape of a flower calyx.

不(示意图)

第二单元

一 丁 丆 不
1　　2　　3　　4

楷书书写顺序

本义指花萼。引申为否定、没有、假设、否、花托等义。

The original meaning refers to a flower calyx and is extended to signify negation, absence, assumption, denial, and flower receptacle, among other meanings.

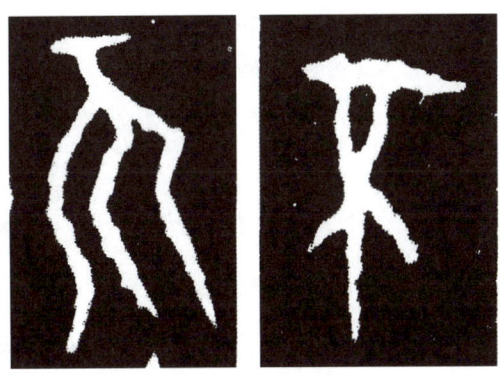

不（甲骨文拓片）

与不组合的词有：不会、不知、不好、不敢、不要、不一定等。

Compound words related to the character "不" include:

1. 不会（bù huì）– Cannot; Will not
2. 不知（bù zhī）– Do not know; Unaware
3. 不好（bù hǎo）– Not good; Unpleasant
4. 不敢（bù gǎn）– Dare not; Not dare to
5. 不要（bù yào）– Do not want; Do not need
6. 不一定（bù yī dìng）– Not necessarily

第二单元

tǔ

土

甲骨文"土"字,像从地上凸起来的土堆形,或像一个土堆的匡廓,旁侧带点者乃表示土屑。应是古代原始的祭社情形,故也为"社"之初文。属象形字。

The Oracle Bone Script character "土" is a pictographic character that resembles the shape of soil or a raised earth mound. It can also represent the outline of a soil heap, with a dot on the side indicating soil particles. This character most likely originated from ancient rituals related to worshipping deities, hence it is also one of the earliest characters associated with the concept of a social group or community.

土(示意图)

第二单元

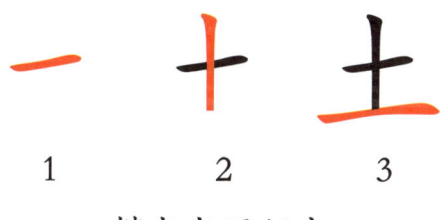

一　十　土
1　　2　　3

楷书书写顺序

本义指聚土以社祭土地神。引申为泥土、家乡、本地的、来自民间的、未开化的、不开通的、领地、田地等义。

The original meaning refers to the gathering of soil for the ritual worship of the Earth deity. It is extended to mean soil, hometown, local, from the people, undeveloped, not accessible, territory, and fields, among other meanings.

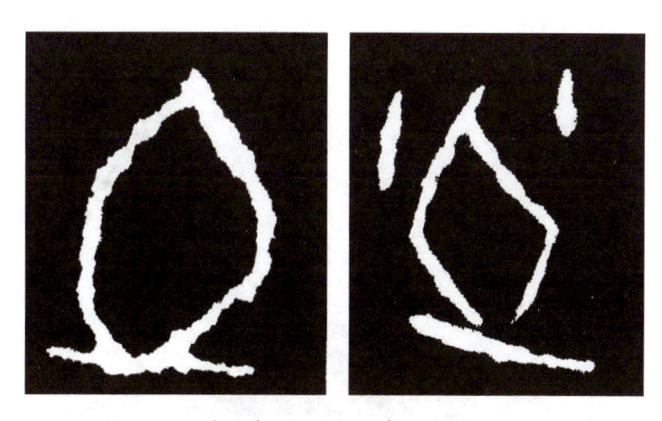

土（甲骨文拓片）

与土组合的词有：土堆、土豆、土墙、土地、土木工程等。
Compound words related to the character "土" include:
1. 土堆（tǔ duī）– Pile of soil
2. 土豆（tǔ dòu）– Potato
3. 土墙（tǔ qiáng）– Earthen wall
4. 土地（tǔ dì）– Land; Earth
5. 土木工程（tǔ mù gōng chéng）– Civil engineering

第二单元

jiā
家

甲骨文"家"字，从宀，像棚屋之形，从豕，像公猪豭之形。可会猪居于棚屋之意。古代在屋子里养猪，有猪就成为有人家的标志。属会意字。

The Oracle Bone Script character "家" consists of the radical "宀"（roof）, representing the shape of a shelter or house, and "豕"（pig）, representing the shape of a male pig or boar. It symbolizes the idea of a pig dwelling in a shelter, indicating that in ancient times, having a pig in the house was a sign of a household. This character belongs to the associative compound character category.

家（示意图）

第二单元

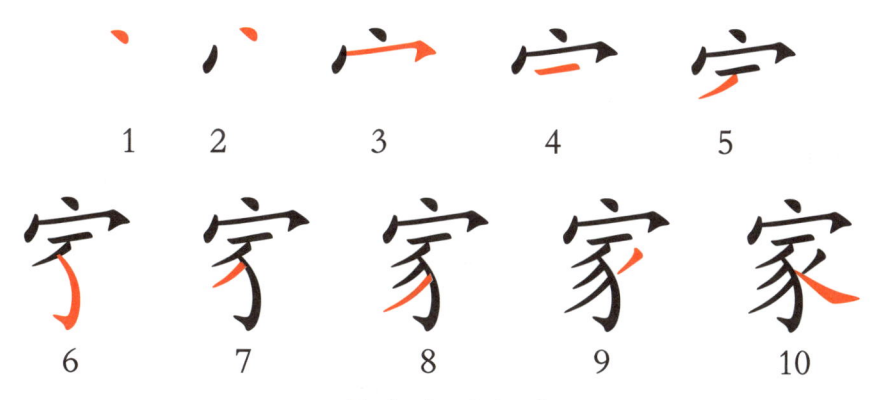

楷书书写顺序

本义指养猪棚。可引申为家庭住所、家庭、家化的、内部的、专家、器物等义。

The original meaning refers to a pigsty. It can be extended to mean residential dwelling, household, domestic, internal, expert, and objects related to a household.

家（甲骨文拓片）

与家组合的词有：家庭、家乡、家具、家族、家乡话等。
Compound words related to the character "家" include:

1. 家庭（jiā tíng）– Family
2. 家乡（jiā xiāng）– Hometown
3. 家具（jiā jù）– Furniture
4. 家族（jiā zú）– Family clan
5. 家乡话（jiā xiāng huà）– Local dialect

mén
门

甲骨文"门"字,像简陋的双扉柴门形。繁体字"門",今汉字简化规范写作"门"为正体。属象形字。

The Oracle Bone Script character "门" depicts a simple double-door wooden gate. The traditional character "門" has been simplified to "门" in modern standard usage. It belongs to the category of pictographic characters.

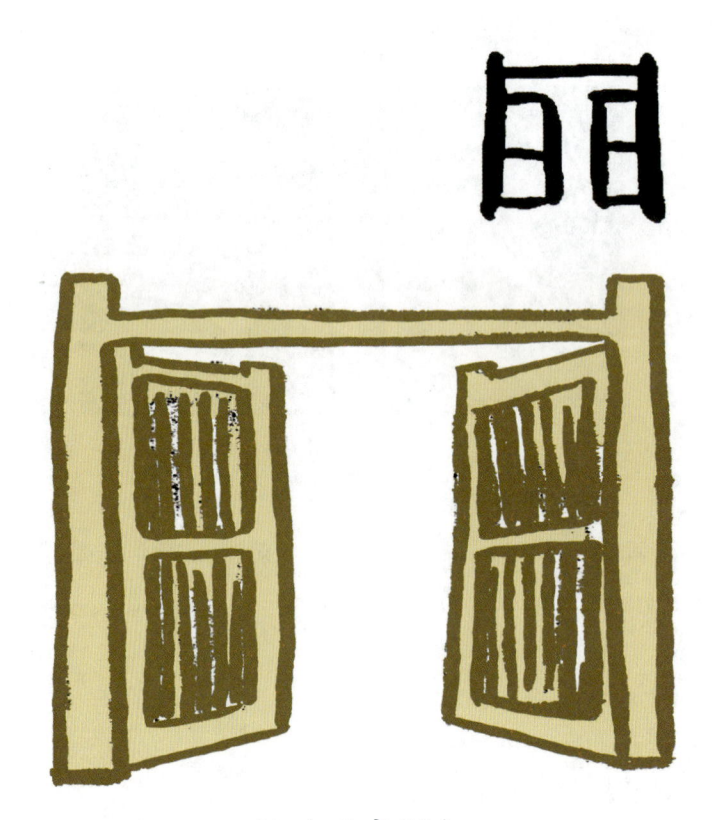

门(示意图)

第二单元

丨 丨 门
1　2　3

楷书书写顺序

本义是指门。可引申为门外、像门的东西、关塞要口、家族、类别、派别、师门、量词等义。

The original meaning refers to a door. It can be extended to mean outside the door, things resembling a door, strategic passes or gates, family lineage, category, faction, school or sect, and a measure word, among other meanings.

门（甲骨文拓片）

与门组合的词有：门窗、门票、门口、门庭若市等。

Compound words related to the character "门" include:

1. 门窗（mén chuāng）– Doors and windows

2. 门票（mén piào）– Entrance ticket

3. 门口（mén kǒu）– Entrance

4. 门庭若市（mén tíng ruò shì）– Bustling with people and activity; Prosperous

第三单元

ér
儿

甲骨文"儿"即"兒"字，头上方中间是开口状，表示婴儿脑囟骨还没有长在一起的意思。又像张口嬉笑露出牙齿之状。属象形字。繁体字"兒"，今汉字简化规范写作"儿"为正体。

The Oracle Bone Script character "儿", also written as "兒", is a pictographic character. The opening in the middle of the head signifies the fontanelle of a baby, indicating that the skull bones have not yet fused together. It also resembles the appearance of a smiling child with an open mouth, showing his teeth. The traditional character "兒" has been simplified to "儿" in modern standard usage.

儿（示意图）

第三单元

丿 儿
1　2
楷书书写顺序

　　本义是指儿童。引申为小孩、儿女等义。古代无论男女都称儿，亦单称青少男子为儿，如：健儿、弄潮儿、孤儿、宠儿、混血儿等。

　　The original meaning refers to a child, and it is extended to mean a small child, son, or daughter. In ancient times, regardless of gender, individuals were referred to as "儿"（ér）. Also, young boys were often called "儿", such as in terms like "健儿"（jiàn'ér—robust youth）, "弄潮儿"（nòng cháo'ér—trendy youth）, "孤儿"（gū'ér—orphan）, "宠儿"（chǒng'ér—beloved child）, "混血儿"（hùn xuè'ér—mixed-race child）, and so on.

儿（甲骨文拓片）

　　与儿组合的词有：儿童、儿子、儿歌、儿女情长等。
　　Compound words related to the character "儿" include:
　　1. 儿童（ér tóng）– Children
　　2. 儿子（ér zi）– Son
　　3. 儿歌（ér gē）– Children's song
　　4. 儿女情长（ér nǚ qíng cháng）– Love between a man and a woman; Romantic love

第三单元

kàn

看

甲骨文"看"字，从目，像眼睛之形。从爪，像一覆手之形。可会手在目上，亦即把手放在眼睛上方，可以遮光望远，集中视线之意。属象形会意字。

The character "看"（kàn）in Oracle Bone Script consists of two components: "目"（mù）meaning "eye" and "爪"（zhuǎ）meaning "claw" or "hand." The character depicts a hand covering the eye, suggesting the act of shading the eyes to look into the distance or focusing one's vision. It is an ideogrammic compound character.

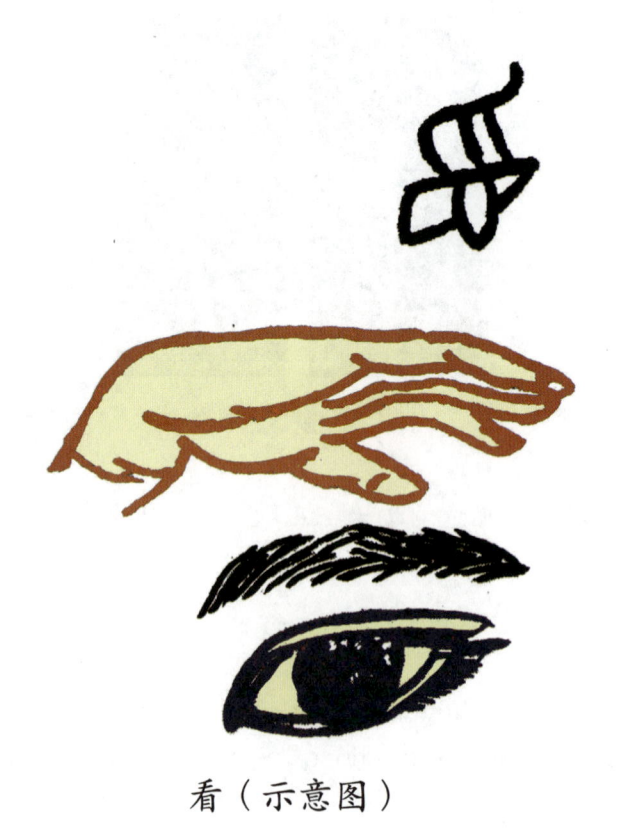

看（示意图）

第三单元

一 二 三 手 看
1　2　3　4　5

看 看 看 看
6　7　8　9

楷书书写顺序

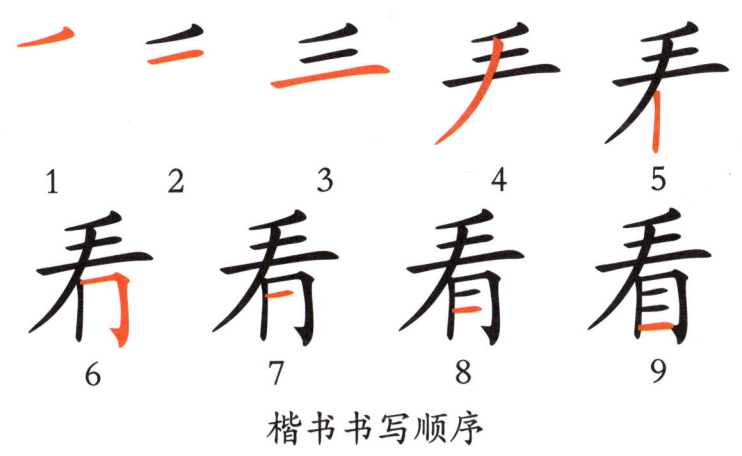

本义为看。引申为观察、探望、料理、估量、照看、尝试、监视、看守等义。

The oracle bone script character "看" originally refers to look and is extended to include meanings such as observe, visit, handle, estimate, take care of, attempt, monitor, guard, etc.

看（甲骨文拓片）

与看组合的词有：看报、看病、看望、看热闹等。

Compound words related to the character "看" include:

1. 看报（kàn bào）– Read a newspaper
2. 看病（kàn bìng）– See a doctor; Seek medical treatment
3. 看望（kàn wàng）– Visit; Call on
4. 看热闹（kàn rè nao）– Watch the excitement; Be a spectator at a lively scene

第三单元

xué

学

（通"敎"）

甲骨文"学"即"學"字，上从两手，像双手摆布算筹的样子，下从爻，视为学字雏形，以表示学习计算；后加屋形、加子字部，以表示在屋子里教孩子学习算术。异体字"敎"加了反文（持棍棒形），以示督责指导之意。今汉字简化规范写作"学"为正体。属会意字。

The character "学" (study), also written as "學", in Oracle Bone Script is depicted with two hands, resembling the gesture of manipulating counting rods. Originally symbolizing learning and calculation, later modifications included the addition of a house shape and the character for "child" to represent teaching children arithmetic in a house. An alternative form, "敎", introduced a reversed character resembling a person holding a stick, indicating supervision and guidance. The modern simplified form is "学", a compound ideogram representing the concept of learning.

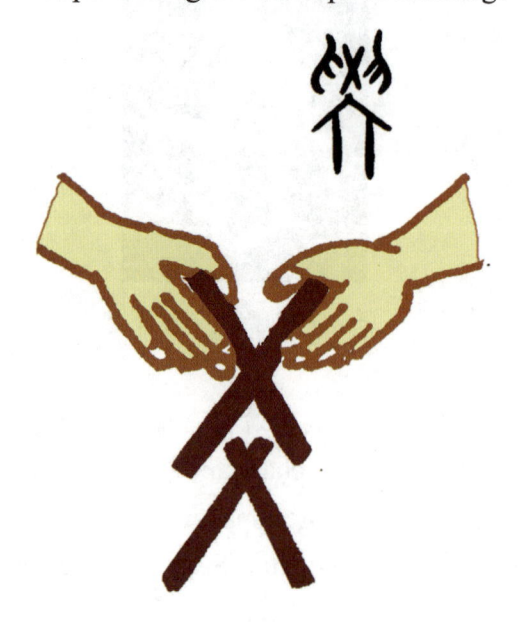

学（示意图）

第三单元

丶 丷 丷 ⺍ ⺌ 学 学 学
1　2　3　4　5　6　7　8

楷书书写顺序

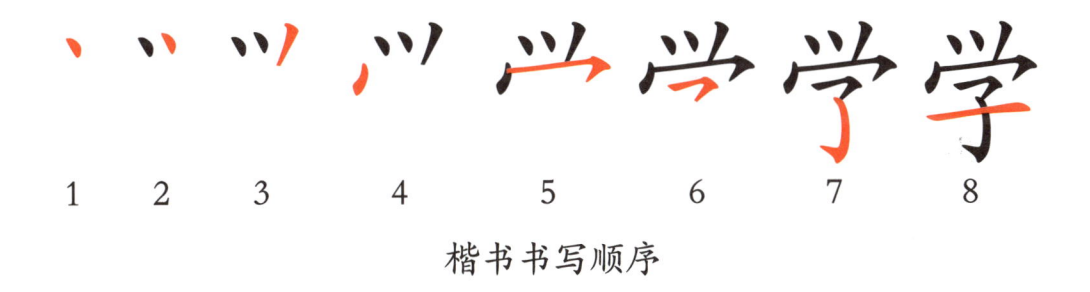

本义指学习。可引申为模仿、学问、学科、学校等义。

The original meaning of "学" refers to study. It can be extended to mean imitation, knowledge, academic disciplines, school, and other related concepts.

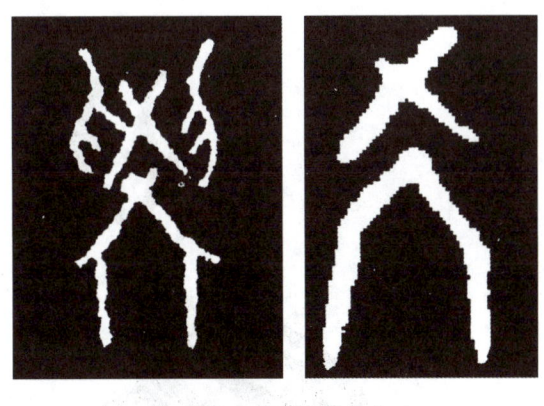

学（甲骨文拓片）

与学组合的词有：学校、学生、学习、学以致用等。
Compound words related to the character "学" include:
1. 学校（xué xiào）– School
2. 学生（xué shēng）– Student
3. 学习（xué xí）– Study; Learn
4. 学以致用（xué yǐ zhì yòng）– Apply what one has learned

jiǔ

酒

　　甲骨文"酒"字,从酉,像酒坛或酒缸之器皿形,并兼表声;从水,表示器皿内之酒水。可会酒器内有酒之意。属形声会意字。

　　The Oracle Bone Script for the character "酒" consists of the radical "酉", resembling a wine jar or vessel, indicating the container for wine, and it includes the element "水", representing the liquid inside the vessel, specifically wine. The combination suggests the concept of wine contained in a vessel. This character belongs to the category of characters known as a pictophonetic compound.

酒(示意图)

第三单元

丶 丶 氵 氵 氵
1　2　3　4　5

汀 沔 沔 沔 酒
6　7　8　9　10

楷书书写顺序

本义是酒。可引申为嗜酒人、醉意、类酒饮料、官名等义。

The original meaning of the character "酒" refers to wine. It can be extended to refer to alcoholics, intoxication, alcoholic beverages, and official titles, among other meanings.

酒（甲骨文拓片）

与酒组合的词有：酒杯、酒瓶、酒席、酒店、酒足饭饱等。

Compound words related to the character "酒" include:

1. 酒杯（jiǔ bēi）– Wine glass
2. 酒瓶（jiǔ píng）– Wine bottle
3. 酒席（jiǔ xí）– Banquet; Feast
4. 酒店（jiǔ diàn）– Hotel
5. 酒足饭饱（jiǔ zú fàn bǎo）– Full of wine and food

第三单元

wén
文
（通"纹"）

甲骨文"文"字，像正立之人形，最上端是头部，向左右伸展的是两臂，下部是两腿，胸前刻有美观的花纹。古以纹为"文"。在身上文身是古代习俗之一，所文之图案各异，或省画不写纹饰而径作文字。属象形字。

The character "文" in Oracle Bone Script resembles an upright human figure. The top part represents the head, and the arms extend to the sides. The bottom part depicts the legs, and there are beautiful patterns carved on the chest. In ancient times, patterns on the body were considered "文"（wen）, and it was a custom to have tattoos. The patterns varied, and sometimes, instead of depicting patterns, characters were directly inscribed. It belongs to the category of pictographic characters.

文（示意图）

第三单元

丶 亠 亍 文
1　2　3　4

楷书书写顺序

本义指文身。可引申为花纹、文章、文献、规律性的现象、华丽文彩、柔和、非军事的、掩饰、裂纹等义。

The original meaning refers to tattoos on the body. Extended meanings include patterns, articles, literature, regular phenomena, beautiful and colorful expressions, softness, non-military, concealment, cracks, etc.

文（甲骨文拓片）

与文组合的词有：文字、文章、文明、文学、文物等。
Compound words related to the character "文" include:
1. 文字（wén zì）– Writing; Characters; Script
2. 文章（wén zhāng）– Article; Essay; Literary works
3. 文明（wén míng）– Civilization; Culture
4. 文学（wén xué）– Literature
5. 文物（wén wù）– Cultural relics

第三单元

shū
书

甲骨文"书"字，上端如人手持笔，下面像是承载书写的器物，古时无纸，只能书刻在龟甲、兽骨、竹片、木板上。两形会意像是手持刀笔在器物上刻写之意。属会意字。繁体字"書"，今汉字简化规范写作"书"为正体。

The original meaning of "书"（shū）in Oracle Bone Script is represented as a compound ideogram. The upper part resembles a hand holding a writing tool, possibly a brush or stylus, while the lower part signifies an object for writing or inscribing, like a tablet or surface. In ancient times when paper was not available, people wrote on materials such as turtle shells, animal bones, bamboo slips, or wooden tablets. The combined imagery suggests the action of holding a writing tool and inscribing on a surface. The traditional form "書" has been simplified to "书" in modern Chinese characters.

书（示意图）

第三单元

乛 㓫 书 书
1   2   3   4

楷书书写顺序

本义是指书写。可引申为文字、字体、书法、书信、文件、书籍等义。

The original meaning of the character "书" (shū) in Oracle Bone Script refers to write or inscribe. It can be extended to mean writing, script, calligraphy, letter, document, book, etc.

书（甲骨文拓片）

与书组合的词有：书写、书法、书店、书房、书包、书香门第等。

Compound words related to the character "书" include:

1. 书写（shū xiě）– Writing
2. 书法（shū fǎ）– Calligraphy
3. 书店（shū diàn）– Bookstore
4. 书房（shū fáng）– Study room
5. 书包（shū bāo）– Schoolbag
6. 书香门第（shū xiāng mén dì）– Family of scholars

sheng

生

甲骨文"生"字,像一棵植物在地上生长出来的样子,下面一横线表示土地,上面三叉形笔画表示草木植物。属象形字。

The Oracle Bone Script for the character "生" resembles the image of a plant growing from the ground, with a horizontal line below representing the soil and three forked strokes above symbolizing vegetation. It belongs to the category of pictographic characters.

生(示意图)

第三单元

丿 亻 与 牛 生
1　2　3　4　5

楷书书写顺序

本义是指草木从土中生长出。可引申为生育、生存、生命、天生的、新鲜的、与"熟"相对的、生疏、生硬、门徒、角色等义。

The original meaning refers to plants growing from the soil. It can be extended to mean give birth, survive, life, innate, fresh, opposite of ripe, unfamiliar, stiff, disciple, role, etc.

生（甲骨文拓片）

与生组合的词有：生长、生活、生态、生命力、生机勃勃等。
Compound words related to the character "生" include:
1. 生长（shēng zhǎng）– Growth
2. 生活（shēng huó）– Life; Livelihood
3. 生态（shēng tài）– Ecology
4. 生命力（shēng mìng lì）– Vitality
5. 生机勃勃（shēng jī bó bó）– Brimming with vitality

第三单元

hé

和

甲骨文"和"即"龢"字,从龠,像排箫编管乐器之形。从禾,本像稻谷禾苗之形,这里作标声,表示乐声和谐之意。属形声字。咊、龢为异体繁书,今汉字简化规范写作"和"为正体。

The character "和" (hé) in Oracle Bone Script is written as "龢", with the component "龠" resembling the shape of a musical instrument, possibly a set of panpipes or reed instruments. The other component "禾" originally depicts the form of rice plants, representing agricultural produce or growth. In this context, it functions as a sound marker, indicating harmony in musical sound. This character belongs to the category of associative sound-meaning characters. The character "和" (hé) in the variant forms "咊" and "龢" has been simplified in modern Chinese writing to the standard form "和".

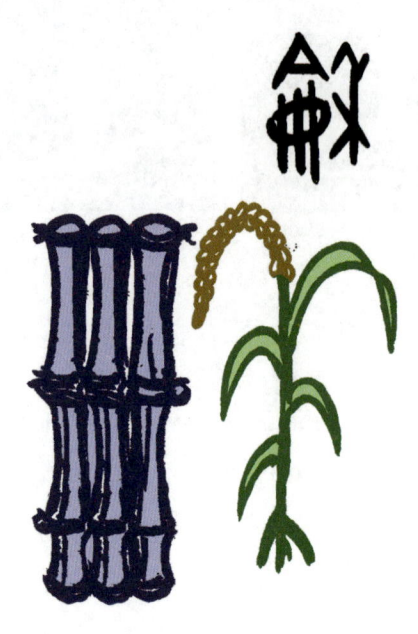

和(示意图)

第三单元

一 二 千 千 禾 禾 和 和
1　2　3　4　5　6　7　8

楷书书写顺序

本义指龠声和谐。可引申为诗词应和、乐声和谐、温和、调和、掺和、和平、众多、结束战争、数学名词等义。

The original meaning refers to the harmonious sound of musical instruments like panpipes or reed instruments. It can be extended to signify poetic and musical harmony, mildness, reconciliation, getting involved, peace, multitude, conclusion of war, and mathematical terms, among other meanings.

和（甲骨文拓片）

与和组合的词有：和平、和解、和谈、和睦、和蔼可亲等。
Compound words related to the character "和" include:
1. 和平（hé píng）– Peace
2. 和解（hé jiě）– Reconciliation
3. 和谈（hé tán）– Peace talks
4. 和睦（hé mù）– Harmony
5. 和蔼可亲（hé ǎi kě qīn）– Kind and amiable

yǒu

有

甲骨文"有"字,像牛头形状,以畜牛为有,以拥有牛表示占有财富,属象形字。后世以借"又"持肉表示有。在上古人看来,有了肉就有了一切,所以,以手持肉就叫作"有",此属会意字。有与"无"相对。

The Oracle Bone Script character "有" resembles the shape of a cow's head, using cattle as a symbol of possession and wealth. It is an ideogram depicting ownership. In later forms, the character borrowed the component "又", representing a hand holding meat, to convey the concept of possession. In ancient times, possessing meat was considered having everything. Thus, the character "有" is a compound ideogram with the hand and meat, signifying possession. It contrasts with the character "无"(wú), meaning "without" or "lacking".

有(示意图)

第三单元

一 𠂇 才 𣎳 有 有
1　2　3　4　5　6

楷书书写顺序

本义是有牛。可引申为存在、发生、客气、丰收、具有、取得、获得、多等义。

The original meaning of the oracle bone script character "有" is having cattle. It can be extended to various meanings such as existence, occurrence, politeness, abundant harvest, possession, acquisition, obtaining, and more.

有（甲骨文拓片）

与有组合的词有：有利、有效、有时候、有意思等。
Compound words related to the character "有" include:
1. 有利（yǒu lì）– Advantageous
3. 有效（yǒu xiào）– Effective
4. 有时候（yǒu shí hòu）– Sometimes
5. 有意思（yǒu yì si）– Interesting

mò

没

（其他读音：méi）

甲骨文"没"字，从水，像水流并带有湍急的漩涡之形；从又，像手之形。可会用手深入水中之意。属象形字。"没"为异体字，今汉字规范写作"没"为正体。

The Oracle Bone Script character "没" depicts flowing water with turbulent whirlpools, accompanied by the shape of a hand. It suggests the act of immersing the hand deeply into the water. This character belongs to the category of pictograms. The variant "没" is another form, and in modern standardized Chinese writing, "没" is the correct form.

没（示意图）

第三单元

丶 丶 氵 氵 沴 没 没
1　2　3　4　5　6　7

楷书书写顺序

本义为用手深入水中。引申为淹没、无、消灭、吞噬、死亡、贪婪等义。

The original meaning is to immerse the hand deeply into the water. It can be extended to imply submersion, non-existence, elimination, engulfment, devouring, death, greed, etc.

有（甲骨文拓片）

与没组合的词有：没完、没事、没用、没错、没想到、没问题等。
Compound words related to the character "没" include:

1. 没完（méi wán）– Not finished
2. 没事（méi shì）– It's nothing
3. 没用（méi yòng）– Useless
4. 没错（méi cuò）– No mistake
5. 没想到（méi xiǎng dào）– Didn't expect
6. 没问题（méi wèn tí）– No problem

第四单元

yuè

月

甲骨文"月"字,像是半月之形。因月亮缺多圆少,故以缺月之形为象。属象形字。

The Oracle Bone Script for the character "月" belongs to the category of pictograms. It resembles the shape of a half moon. Due to the moon being often less than full, the character takes the form of a crescent moon to represent it.

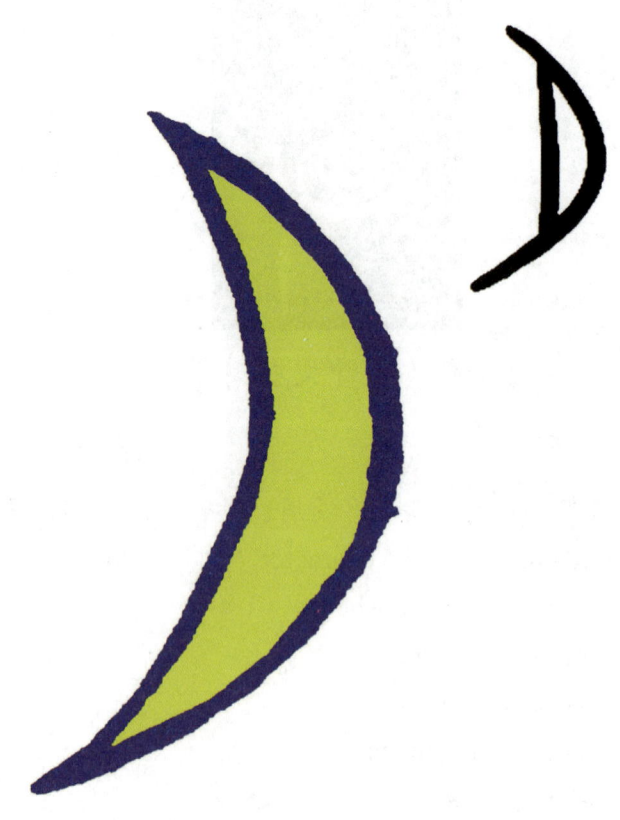

月(示意图)

第四单元

丿 刀 月 月
1　2　3　4
楷书书写顺序

本义是指月亮。可引申为月份、每月、形色像月的东西等义。

The original meaning refers to the moon. It can be extended to mean month, every month, things that resemble the shape or color of the moon, and so on.

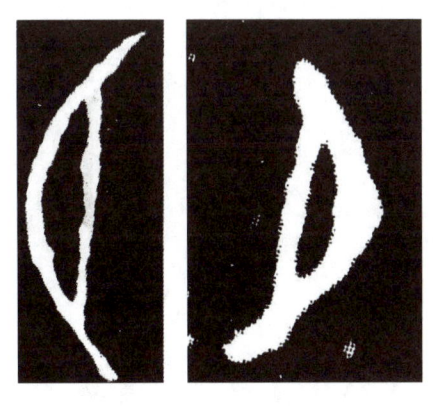

月（甲骨文拓片）

与月组合的词有：月底、月球、月全食等。
Compound words related to the character "月"（yuè）include:
1. 月底（yuè dǐ）– Month-end
2. 月球（yuè qiú）– The moon
3. 月全食（yuè quán shí）– Total lunar eclipse

第四单元

míng

明

甲骨文"明"字，有两种形式，一种左边是从日，右边是从月，表示日月相照，明亮光辉。另一种形式左边是一窗户之象形图，右边还是月，表示月亮从窗户照进来，显得十分明亮之意。属会意字。

The Oracle Bone Script for the character "明" has two forms. In one form, the left side represents the sun, and the right side represents the moon, symbolizing the radiance when the sun and moon shine together, creating bright and brilliant light. In the other form, the left side depicts a pictorial representation of a window, and the right side remains as the moon, indicating the brightness when the moonlight enters through the window, giving a sense of vivid illumination. It belongs to the category of compound ideogram characters.

明（示意图）

第四单元

丨 冂 冂 日 日 日) 明 明 明
1　2　3　4　5　6　7　8

楷书书写顺序

本义是光亮、明亮。可引申为天亮、点燃、点亮、了解、眼睛、视力、白昼、明白、明显、明智、明艳、明眼、公开、清楚等义。

The original meaning of the character "明" is brightness or luminosity. It can be extended to signify dawn, ignite, illuminate, understand, eyes, vision, daytime, clarity, obviousness, wisdom, brightness（of colors）, keen-eyed, public, and clear, among other meanings.

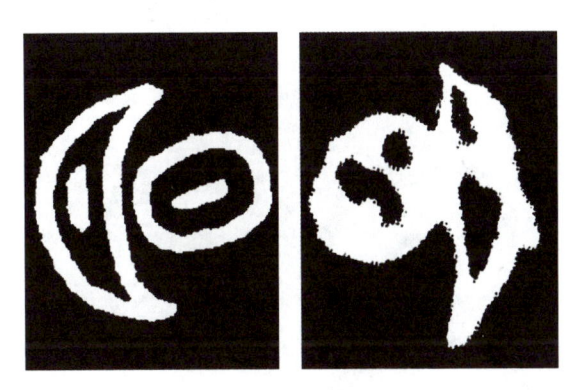

明（甲骨文拓片）

与明组合的词有：明年、明晰、明显、明明白白等。
Compound words related to the character "明" include:
1. 明年（míng nián）– Next year
2. 明晰（míng xī）– Clear and distinct
3. 明显（míng xiǎn）– Obvious
4. 明明白白（míng míng bái bái）– Clearly and plainly

第四单元

péng

朋

甲骨文"朋"字,像是两串贝串连在一起之形。贝是古代一种货币单位,即五贝为一串,而两串为一朋。属象形字。

The Oracle Bone Script for the character "朋" depicts the image of two strings of cowrie shells linked together. Cowrie shells were an ancient currency unit, with five shells forming a string, and two strings constituting one unit, represented by the character "朋". This character belongs to the category of pictograms.

朋(示意图)

第四单元

丿 刀 月 月 月 朋 朋 朋
1　2　3　4　5　6　7　8

楷书书写顺序

本义是指古代贝币单位。可引申为朋友、群结、勾结、朋党等义。

The original meaning of the character "朋" refers to the ancient cowrie shell currency unit. It can be extended to mean friend, a group or association, forming a close bond, collusion, political faction, and so on.

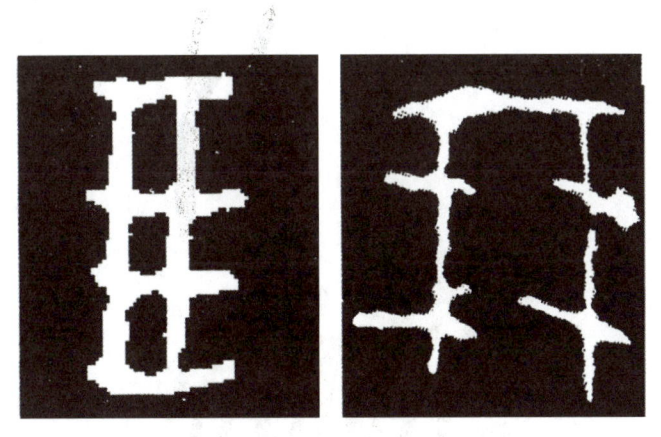

朋（甲骨文拓片）

与朋组合的词有：朋友、朋辈、高朋满座等。
Compound words related to the character "朋" include:
1. 朋友（péng you）— Friend
2. 朋辈（péng bèi）— Peers or colleagues
3. 高朋满座（gāo péng mǎn zuò）— A gathering of distinguished guests

67

yǒu
友

　　甲骨文"友"字，是相向的两只右手并列在一起，表示共同做事，与朋友志同道合之义。古代同志曰友，同门曰朋。属会意字。

　　The Oracle Bone Script for the character "友" features two right hands facing each other and placed side by side, symbolizing collaborative efforts and the shared aspirations of friends. In ancient times, comrades with similar aspirations were referred to as "友", while those of the same school or discipline were called "朋". This character belongs to the category of compound ideogram characters.

友（示意图）

第四单元

一 ナ 方 友
1　2　3　4

楷书书写顺序

本义指朋友。引申为相好、亲近、互相合作等义。

The original meaning of the character "友" is friend. It can be extended to mean getting along well, being close, and cooperating with each other.

友（甲骨文拓片）

与友组合的词有：友好、友谊、友情、友善、良师益友等。

Compound words related to the character "友" include:

1. 友好（yǒu hǎo）– Friendly
2. 友谊（yǒu yì）– Friendship
3. 友情（yǒu qíng）– Friendship
4. 友善（yǒu shàn）– Kind and friendly
5. 良师益友（liáng shī yì yǒu）– Good teachers and helpful friends

第四单元

shàng

上

甲骨文"上"字,是在一长横或一长带弯弧线(象征物体)上部加一短横(象征物体),可g表意专指物体上部的物体,表明位置在上方。属指事字。

The Oracle Bone Script character "上" is formed by adding a short horizontal line (symbolizing an object) above a long horizontal line or a long line with a curved arc (symbolizing an object). This configuration specifically denotes an object located on the upper part of another object, indicating a sense of position being above. It belongs to the category of indicative characters.

上(示意图)

第四单元

丨 卜 上
1　2　3

楷书书写顺序

本义是指上端、高处。可引申为上面的、地位高的、事物表层的、向上走、按时参与、进献、添加、登记、达到、趋向、结果等义。

The original meaning of the character "上" refers to the upper part or a high position. It can be extended to mean on top, of higher status, the surface of things, moving upward, participating in a timely manner, contributing, adding, registering, reaching, trending toward, result, etc.

上（甲骨文拓片）

与上组合的词有：上海、上午、上网、上下班、上进心等。

Compound words related to the character "上" include:

1. 上海（shàng hǎi）- Shanghai
2. 上午（shàng wǔ）- Morning
3. 上网（shàng wǎng）- Go online
4. 上下班（shàng xià bān）- Commute to and from work
5. 上进心（shàng jìn xīn）- Aspiration for progress

71

第四单元

xià

下

甲骨文"下"字,是在一长横或一长带弯弧线(象征物体)下部加一短横(象征物体),可表意专指物体下部的物体,表明位置在下方。属指事字。

The Oracle Bone Script for the character "下" is formed by adding a short horizontal line (symbolizing an object) below a long horizontal line or a long line with a curved arc (symbolizing an object). This configuration specifically denotes an object located in the lower part of another object, indicating a sense of position being below. It belongs to the category of indicative characters.

下(示意图)

第四单元

一 丅 下
1　2　3

楷书书写顺序

　　本义是指事物的位置在低处的。后引申为低级的、次品的、次序在后位的、所属的、低于、少于、走下、落下、去、到、离开、退出、次数、动作趋向、放下架子等义。

The Oracle Bone Script character "下" originally signifies the position of something being at a lower place. It later extends to mean lower level, inferior quality, in a lower position in order, belonging to, below, less than, descend, fall down, go to, arrive, leave, exit, frequency, the direction of an action, putting aside pretense, and so on.

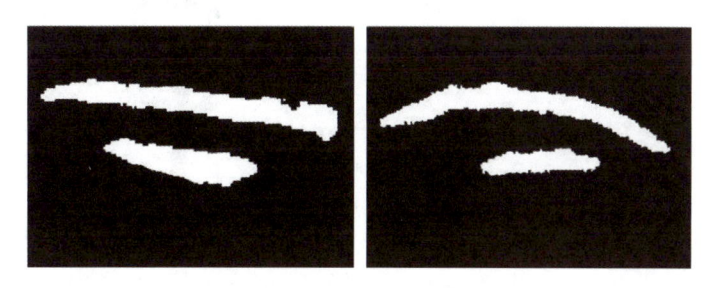

下（甲骨文拓片）

　　与下组合的词有：下面、下来、下班、下降、下车、下星期等。
Compound words related to the character "下" include:
1. 下面（xià miàn）– Below; Underneath
2. 下来（xià lái）– Come down; Descend
3. 下班（xià bān）– Off work; Finish work
4. 下降（xià jiàng）– Descend; Decline
5. 下车（xià chē）– Get off the vehicle
6. 下星期（xià xīng qī）– Next week

第四单元

zǎo

早

甲骨文"早"字,从日,像太阳之形;从甲,像龟甲开裂或东西破裂状。两形会意表示天将破晓、太阳冲破黑暗而裂开涌出之意。

The Oracle Bone Script character "早" is composed of two parts: "日"（sun）and "甲"（turtle shell）. The "日" part represents the sun, and the "甲" part resembles a cracked turtle shell or the state of something breaking. The combination of these two forms signifies the dawn, as the sun breaks through the darkness, symbolizing the emergence of light.

早（示意图）

第四单元

丨 冂 曰 日 旦 早

1　2　3　4　5　6

楷书书写顺序

本义为早晨，指从天亮到早上七八点钟的一段时间，如早饭、早操、早课、早膳、早霞等，皆指早事。引申泛指时间靠前的、比一定时间提前的。又指在平生的早期、在年轻时，以及幸亏等义。

The original meaning of the character "早" is the morning, referring to the period from dawn until around seven or eight in the morning. Terms such as breakfast, morning exercises, morning classes, early meals, and morning glow all denote activities in the morning. It is extended to broadly refer to things or events that occur earlier than a certain time. It also indicates early stages in one's life, during youth, and carries the meaning of "fortunately" or "thanks to".

早（甲骨文拓片）

与早组合的词有：早期、早餐、早茶、早有所闻等。
Compound words related to the character "早" include:
1. 早期（zǎo qī）– Early stage
2. 早餐（zǎo cān）– Breakfast
3. 早茶（zǎo chá）– Morning tea
4. 早有所闻（zǎo yǒu suǒ wén）– Heard about it early on

第四单元

wǔ

午

甲骨文"午"字，像束丝交午之形，为午字初形。属象形字。甲骨文"午"通"玄""幺"字。

The Oracle Bone Script character "午" resembles the intertwining of bundled threads, depicting a woven pattern and representing the earliest form of the character "午". It belongs to the category of pictograms. In Oracle Bone Script, the character "午" is often used interchangeably with the characters "玄" and "幺".

午（示意图）

第四单元

ノ 亻 匕 午
1　2　3　4

楷书书写顺序

本义是指束丝交午。可引申为纵横相交、戳等义。也表示日中的时候、白天十二点、借用作地支第七位。

The original meaning of the character "午" refers to the intertwining of bundled threads. It can be extended to mean interweaving, and poking or stabbing, among other meanings. It also represents midday, twelve o'clock in the daytime, the seventh of the Earthly Branches.

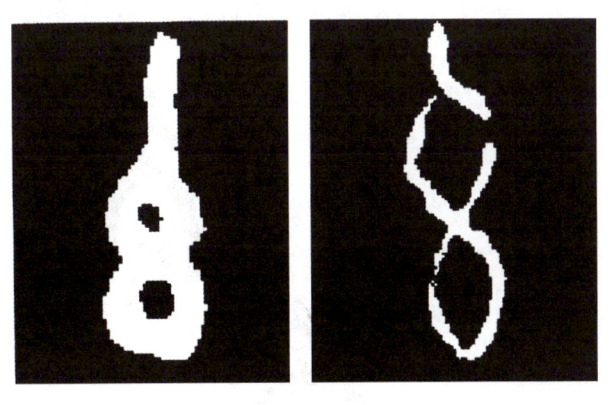

午（甲骨文拓片）

与午组合的词有：午后、午餐、午睡、下午茶、子午线等。

Compound words related to the character "午" include:

1. 午后（wǔ hòu）– Afternoon
2. 午餐（wǔ cān）– Lunch
3. 午睡（wǔ shuì）– Afternoon nap
4. 下午茶（xià wǔ chá）– Afternoon tea
5. 子午线（zǐ wǔ xiàn）– Meridian; Prime meridian

第四单元

qù

去

甲骨文"去"字，上部大字代表人，下部从口，或从口字去掉上横，像一凹口之形，与口无别，指洞穴口、门口，或代表坎陷，表示人离开洞穴或跨越坎陷之谓，以会远离之意。属会意字。

The Oracle Bone Script character "去" consists of the "大" character on the top representing a person and a component below formed from the "口" character. The lower part either includes the full "口" character or omits the upper horizontal stroke, forming a concave shape similar to a depressed mouth. This shape is indistinguishable from the character "口" and refers to the entrance of a cave, a doorway, or symbolizes a depression. It signifies a person leaving a cave or crossing over an obstacle, indicating the idea of moving away. This character belongs to the category of compound ideogram characters.

去（示意图）

第四单元

一　十　土　去　去
1　　2　　3　　4　　5

楷书书写顺序

　　本义是指，与"来"相对，离开。可引申为距离、过去的、前往、趋向、去掉等义。

　　The original meaning of the character "去" refers to leave. It can be extended to mean distance, the past, go to, tendency, store, remove, among other meanings.

去（甲骨文拓片）

　　与去组合的词有：去向、去年、去伪存真等。
Compound words related to the character "去" include:
1. 去向（qù xiàng）– Whereabouts; Direction
2. 去年（qù nián）– Last year
3. 去伪存真（qù wěi cún zhēn）– Eliminate the false and retain the true

第四单元

yào

要

甲骨文"要"字，中间从女，像一妇女侧视形。两边从爪，像双手叉腰（或双手指腰）之形。中部上方从日，原本指太阳，此表示人之头部。可会双手叉腰之意，当是"腰"之本字。属象形会意字。

The Oracle Bone Script character "要" consists of a central element derived from the character "女"（woman），resembling the profile of a woman in a side view. On both sides, there are elements derived from "爪"（claw），resembling hands placed on the waist or forming a gesture of hands on the waist. Above the central part, there is an element derived from "日"（sun），originally representing the sun, but here indicating the head of a person. The entire character signifies the gesture of hands on the waist, likely representing the original form for the character "腰"（waist）. This character belongs to the category of compound ideogram characters.

要（示意图）

第四单元

1 2 3 4 5

6 7 8 9

楷书书写顺序

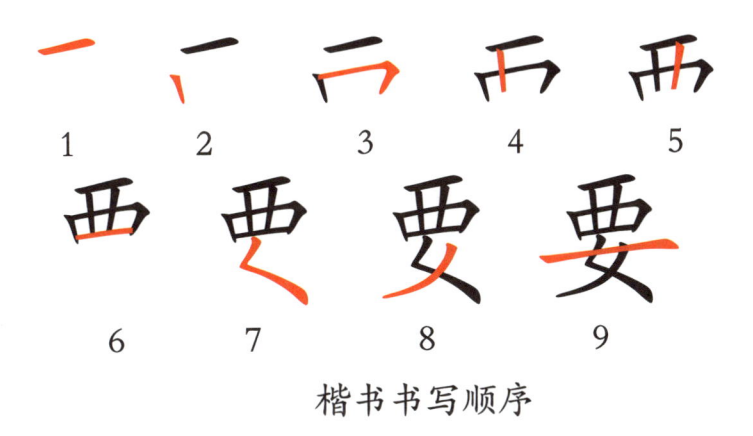

本义指腰。引申为重要、想、希望、总、讨、叫、让、将要、如果等义。
The original meaning of the character "要" refers to waist. It is extended to mean important, think, hope, overall, ask for, call, let, will, if, and so on.

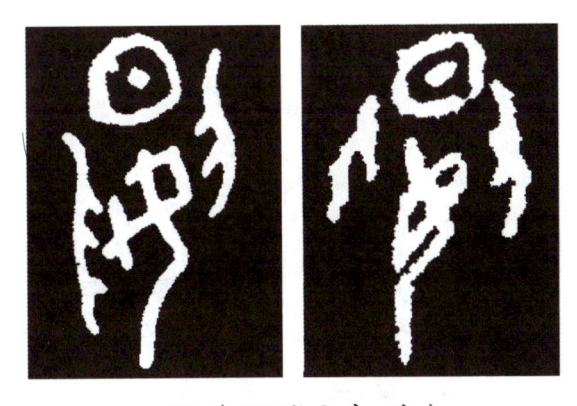

要（甲骨文拓片）

与要组合的词有：要素、要害、要求、要不然等。
Compound words related to the character "要" include:
1. 要素（yào sù）– Element; Factor
2. 要害（yào hài）– Key point; Crucial part
3. 要求（yāo qiú）– Demand; Requirement
4. 要不然（yào bù rán）– Otherwise

第五单元

yī

一

甲骨文"一"字,皆以一横表示其形态,是古人记数形式之一,无特定意义。也用手势比画表数。属指事字。

The Oracle Bone Script character "一" is a symbol indicating number, primarily represented by a horizontal stroke. It served as one of the ancient numerical notations without a specific meaning. People in ancient times also used gestures or drawings to convey numerical information. This character belongs to the category of indicative characters.

一(示意图)

第五单元

一

1
楷书书写顺序

本义指数始一。引申为少数、同一、满、全、统一、专一、每、乃等义。

The original meaning of the character "一" is the beginning of counting. It is extended to mean few, the same, full, whole, unified, specialized, every, and therefore, among other meanings.

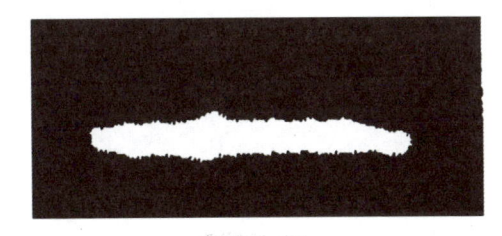

一（甲骨文拓片）

与一组合的词有：一生、一直、一天、一半、一定、一家人等。

Compound words related to the character "一" include:

1. 一生（yì shēng）– Lifetime
2. 一直（yī zhí）– Continuously; Straight
3. 一天（yī tiān）– One day
4. 一半（yī bàn）– Half
5. 一定（yī dìng）– Definitely; Certain
6. 一家人（yī jiā rén）– Whole family

第五单元

èr

二

甲骨文"二"字，为数目字，出自算筹，一加一所得。用二指手势比画，亦以两筹码或两横来表示数目二。属指事字。

The Oracle Bone Script character "二" represents the number two, indicating the result of adding one and one together. It is derived from counting or calculating. This character is a pictogram and is represented either by a hand gesture with two fingers or by using two tallies or horizontal lines to signify the numerical value of two.

二（示意图）

第五单元

二

1　　　2

楷书书写顺序

本义指数目序数二。引申为第二、双、两样、比并、再次、不专一等义。

The original meaning of the character "二" is the ordinal number two. It is extended to mean second, pair, two kinds, comparison and combining, again, lack of specificity, and so on.

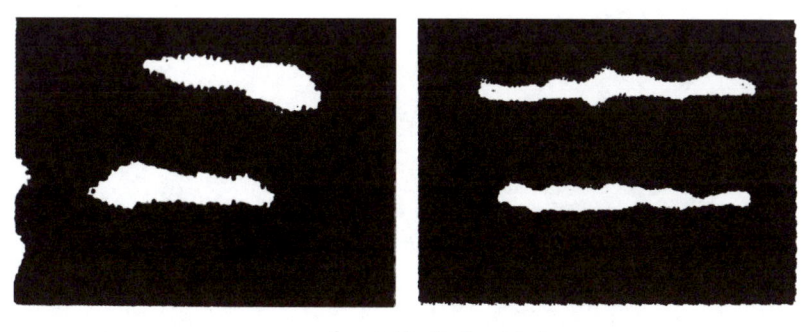

二（甲骨文拓片）

与二组合的词有：二月、二重唱、二氧化碳等。

Compound words related to the character "二" include:

1. 二月（èr yuè）– February
2. 二重唱（èr chóng chàng）– Duet
3. 二氧化碳（èr yǎng huà tàn）– Carbon dioxide

第五单元

sān

三

甲骨文"三"字，为数目字，出自算筹，二加一所得。其构型以伸三指手势比画，卜文用三横表示。属指事字。

The Oracle Bone Script character "三" is a pictogram representing the number three. It originates from counting or calculating, specifically as the result of adding two and one together. The character's configuration is based on the gesture of extending three fingers, and in divination inscriptions, it is represented by three horizontal lines.

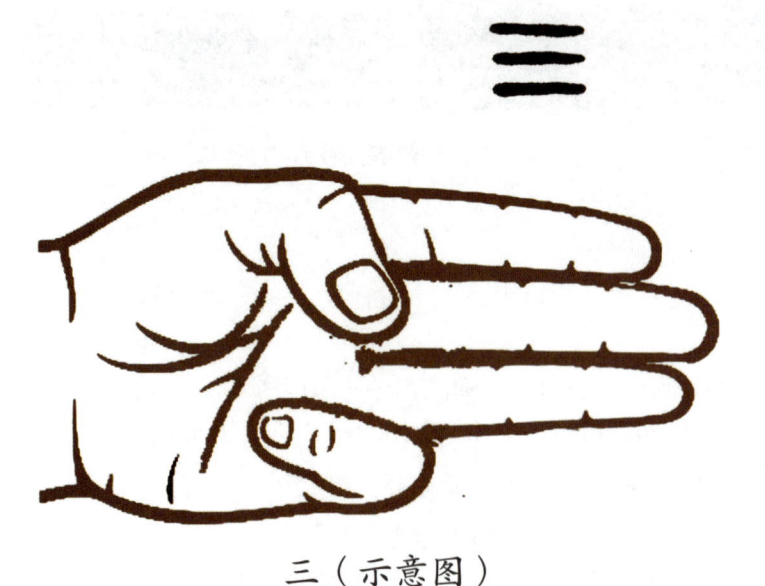

三（示意图）

第五单元

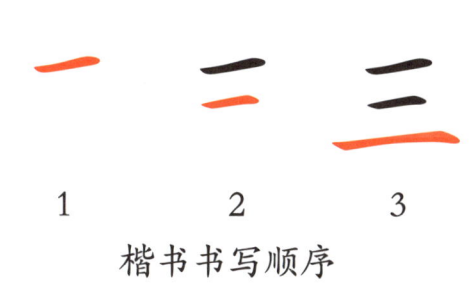

一 二 三
1   2   3
楷书书写顺序

本义指数目序数三。引申为多数、再三、三番五次等义。

The original meaning of the character "三" is the ordinal number three. It is extended to mean a majority, repeatedly, and many times.

三（甲骨文拓片）

与三组合的词有：三伏、三峡、三角形、三言两语、三思而行等。

Compound words related to the character "三" include:

1. 三伏（sān fú）– The three periods of hottest summer days
2. 三峡（sān xiá）– Three Gorges（refers to the Three Gorges region along the Yangtze River）
3. 三角形（sān jiǎo xíng）– Triangle
4. 三言两语（sān yán liǎng yǔ）– A few words; Brief remarks
5. 三思而行（sān sī ér xíng）– Think twice before you act

sì

四

甲骨文"四"字,为数目字,出自算筹,三加一所得。常以手势伸出四指比画为记数,卜文以四横画表示。春秋战国后,写作"口"内"八"字形。

The Oracle Bone Script character "四" is a numerical symbol representing the number four. It originates from counting or calculating, specifically as the result of adding three and one together. It is often represented by the gesture of extending four fingers for counting, and in divination inscriptions, it is symbolized by four horizontal lines.

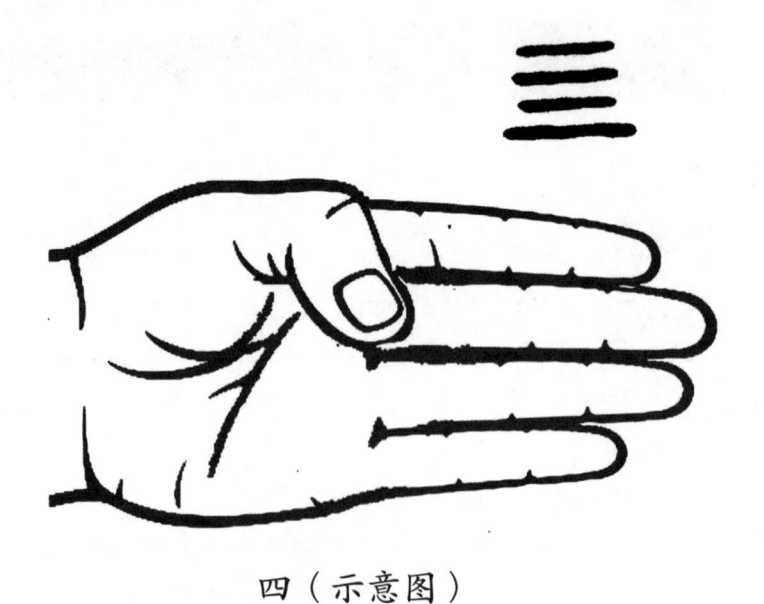

四(示意图)

第五单元

丨 冂 冂 四 四
1　2　3　4　5

楷书书写顺序

本义指数目四。引申为第四、大等义。

The original meaning of the character "四" is the ordinal number four. It is extended to mean the fourth, significant size, and other related meanings.

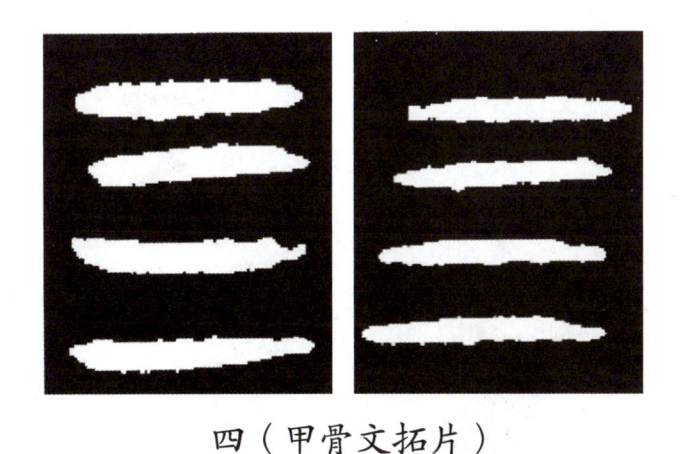

四（甲骨文拓片）

与四组合的词有：四海、四角、四方形、四面八方、四季如春等。

Compound words related to the character "四" include:

1. 四海（sì hǎi）– The four seas; Everywhere
2. 四角（sì jiǎo）– Four corners
3. 四方形（sì fāng xíng）– Square
4. 四面八方（sì miàn bā fāng）– All sides; All directions
5. 四季如春（sì jì rú chūn）– Spring-like all year round

第五单元

wǔ

五

甲骨文"五"字,像两物交叉之形。上下横表示天地,乂表示阴阳二气在天地间交错。属象形字。

The Oracle Bone Script character "五" is a pictogram representing the number five. It is a symbolic depiction of two objects crossing each other. The horizontal lines at the top and bottom represent heaven and earth, while the intersecting line in the middle represents the intertwining of the two cosmic forces of *yin* and *yang* between heaven and earth.

五(示意图)

第五单元

一 厂 五 五
1　2　3　4

楷书书写顺序

本义指纵横交错。后假借为数目五。

The original meaning of the character "五" is the intertwining of vertical and horizontal lines. Later, it was borrowed to represent the numerical value five.

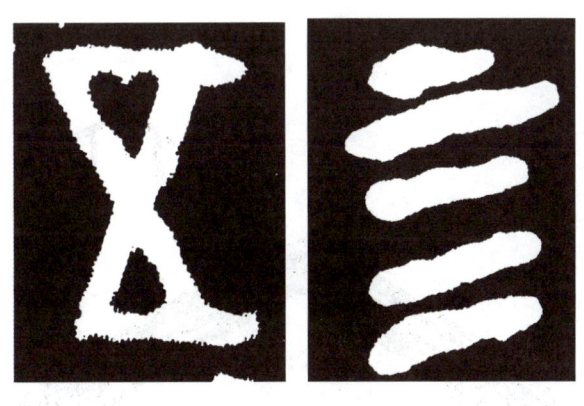

五（甲骨文拓片）

与五组合的词有：五月、五线谱、五谷丰登、五彩缤纷等。

Compound words related to the character "五" include:

1. 五月（wǔ yuè）– May
2. 五线谱（wǔ xiàn pǔ）– Musical staff; Stave
3. 五谷丰登（wǔ gǔ fēng dēng）– Abundant harvest of the five grains
4. 五彩缤纷（wǔ cǎi bīn fēn）– Colorful and dazzling

第五单元

liù

六

甲骨文"六"字,像原始茅庐状,类近宝盖头写法。借作记数用字六。卜辞用作数词、序词。属象形字。

The Oracle Bone Script character "六" resembles the primitive shape of a thatched hut, similar to the "treasure cap" style of writing. It was borrowed and adapted as a numerical character for counting and as an ordinal number in divination inscriptions. This character belongs to the category of pictograms.

六(示意图)

第五单元

丶 一 亠 六
1　2　3　4

楷书书写顺序

本义指棚庐。后假借为数目六。

The original meaning of the character "六" is a thatched hut or shelter, and it is extended to represent the number six.

六（甲骨文拓片）

与六组合的词有：六月、六边形、六弦琴等。

Compound words related to the character "六" include:

1. 六月（liù yuè）– June
2. 六边形（liù biān xíng）– Hexagon
3. 六弦琴（liù xián qín）– Six-stringed musical instrument

第五单元

qī

七

甲骨文"七"字,表示切断一根棍棒。属指事字。

The Oracle Bone Script character "七" is a pictogram representing the action of cutting a stick or rod.

七(示意图)

第五单元

七

1　2

楷书书写顺序

本义为切。后假借为数目七。

The original meaning of the character "七" refers to cut and it is extended and borrowed to represent the numerical value seven.

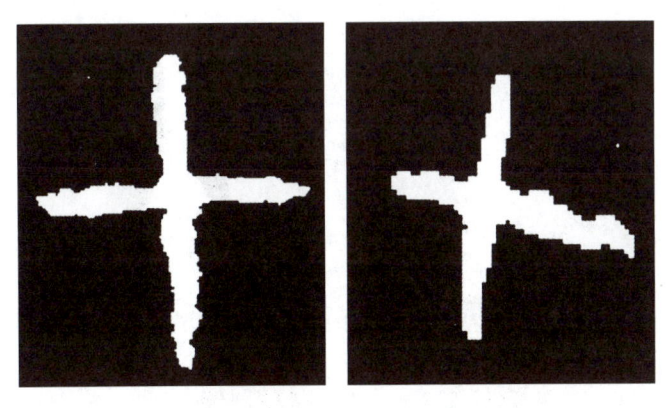

七（甲骨文拓片）

与七组合的词有：七月、七彩、七上八下等。

Compound words related to the character "七" include:

1. 七月（qī yuè）– July
2. 七彩（qī cǎi）– Seven colors; Colorful
3. 七上八下（qī shàng bā xià）– Nervous or agitated（literally, "seven up, eight down"）

第五单元

bā

八

甲骨文"八"字,用两画相背来表明将一物剖解分开之意。八字被借作数词。属指事会意字。

The Oracle Bone Script character "八" is a pictogram representing the act of splitting or dividing something into two parts. The character "八" is borrowed to serve as a numerical character. It belongs to the category of compound ideogram characters.

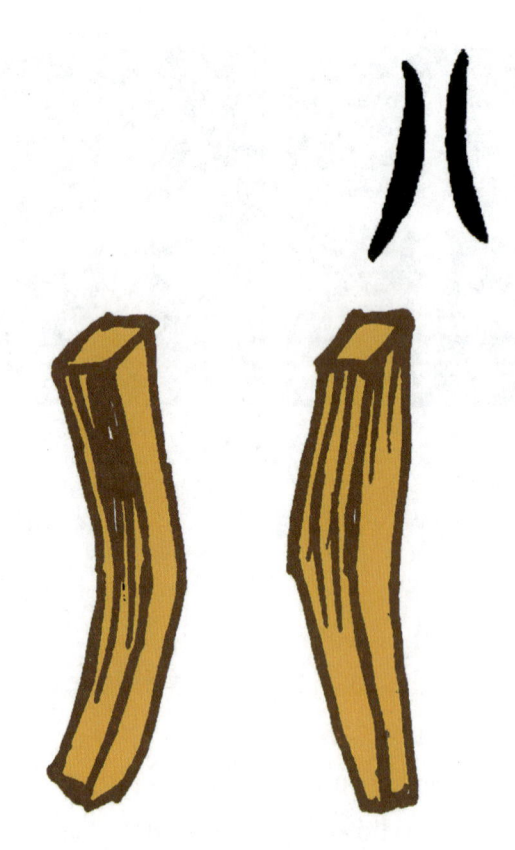

八(示意图)

第五单元

丿 ㇏
1　2
楷书书写顺序

本义是指将物区分开。可引申为分开、七加一的和等义。

The original meaning of the character "八" is to separate or distinguish between things. It is extended to mean division or separation and is also used to represent the sum of seven and one.

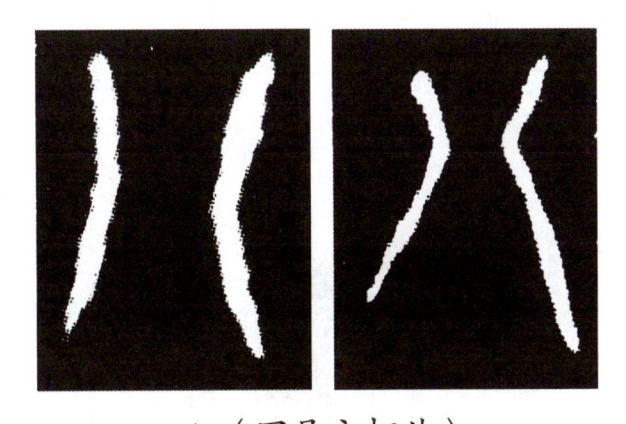

八（甲骨文拓片）

与八组合的词有：八月、八方支援、八面玲珑等。
Compound words related to the character "八" include:
1. 八月（bā yuè）– August
2. 八方支援（bā fāng zhī yuán）– Support from all directions
3. 八面玲珑（bā miàn líng lóng）– Versatile; Resourceful

97

第五单元

jiǔ

九

甲骨文"九"字,本为象形字。左边像虫头,右边像虫向上曲屈之尾的形状。另说像兽类的尾巴处加一撇画,以表示指事符号,专指尾巴根处。后借作数字九。

The Oracle Bone Script character "九" is originally a pictogram. The left part resembles the head of an insect, and the right part represents the upward-curving tail of the insect. Another interpretation suggests that it resembles the tail of an animal with an added stroke at the base, specifically indicating the root of the tail. It is borrowed to represent the numerical value nine.

九(示意图)

第五单元

丿 九
1　2
楷书书写顺序

本义指尾巴。后其本义消亡，引申假借为数目字、时令名、泛指多等义。古人造字纪数，起于一，极于九，九是最大的个位数。古代社会生活中，凡形容极高、极大、极广、极远的事物，都用"九"。

The original meaning of the character "九" is the tail. Later, its original meaning faded. It is extended and borrowed to represent numerical values, names of seasons, and the general concept of plenty. In ancient times, when people created characters for counting, it started with one and culminated with nine, which is the largest single-digit number. In the social life of ancient times, the term "九" was used to describe things that were extremely high, large, broad, or distant.

九（甲骨文拓片）

与九组合的词有：九州、九寨沟、九霄云外、九牛一毛等。
Compound words related to the character "九" include:

1. 九州（jiǔ zhōu）– Nine provinces（referring to the traditional divisions of China）

2. 九寨沟（Jiǔ zhài gōu）– Jiuzhaigou Valley（a scenic area in Sichuan Province）

3. 九霄云外（jiǔ xiāo yún wài）– Beyond the ninth heaven and clouds（figuratively, something extremely distant）

4. 九牛一毛（jiǔ niú yī máo）– Nine cows and one strand of cow hair（figuratively, a tiny amount compared to something much larger）

第五单元

shí

十

甲骨文"十"字,像是一条竖形状直线。古用一根树棍代表十,或特指一根有刻度的木棍,后则演变为中间加一短横。而甲骨文就用"丨"来表示十。属指事字。

The Oracle Bone Script character "十" is a pictogram and belongs to the category of compound ideogram characters. It resembles a straight vertical line. In ancient times, ten was represented by a single tree branch, or specifically, a marked wooden stick. Later, it evolved to have a short horizontal line in the middle. In Oracle Bone Script, "丨" was used to represent the concept of ten.

十(示意图)

第五单元

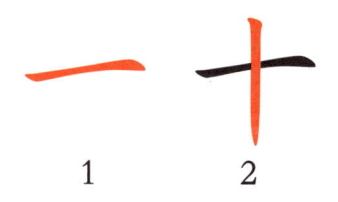

十

1　2

楷书书写顺序

本义是数目十。引申为完善、完满、等分为十、程度深、数量足或一个约数等义。

The original meaning of the character "十" is the numerical value ten. It is extended to mean completeness, perfection, being divided into ten parts, depth or degree of something, sufficient quantity, or a rough estimate.

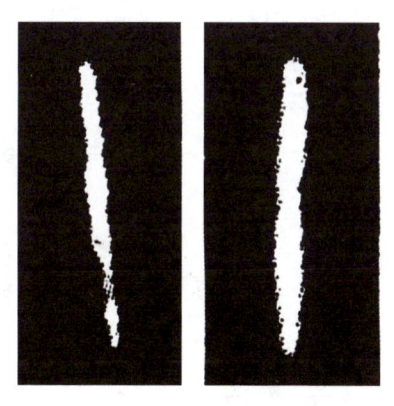

十（甲骨文拓片）

与十组合的词有：十一月、十字架、十二生肖、十万火急、十全十美、十字路口等。

Compound words related to the character "十" include:

1. 十一月（shí yī yuè）– November（the eleventh month）

2. 十字架（shí zì jià）– Cross（as in a crucifix）

3. 十二生肖（shí èr shēng xiào）– Twelve Chinese zodiac signs

4. 十万火急（shí wàn huǒ jí）– Extremely urgent（literally "a hundred thousand urgent fires"）

5. 十全十美（shí quán shí měi）– Perfect in every way（literally "ten complete, ten beautiful"）

6. 十字路口（shí zì lù kǒu）– Crossroad; Intersection

第六单元

měi
美

甲骨文"美"字，像一个正面站立之人，头上有羽毛或羊角一样的饰物，表示形貌美丽好看。属象形会意字。

The Oracle Bone Script character "美" depicts a person standing frontally, with an ornament resembling feathers or horns on the head, symbolizing a beautiful and attractive appearance. It belongs to the category of compound ideogram characters with both pictorial and associative elements.

美（示意图）

第六单元

`丶 丷 䒑 䒑 䒑`
1　2　3　4　5

`羊 羊 美 美`
6　7　8　9

楷书书写顺序

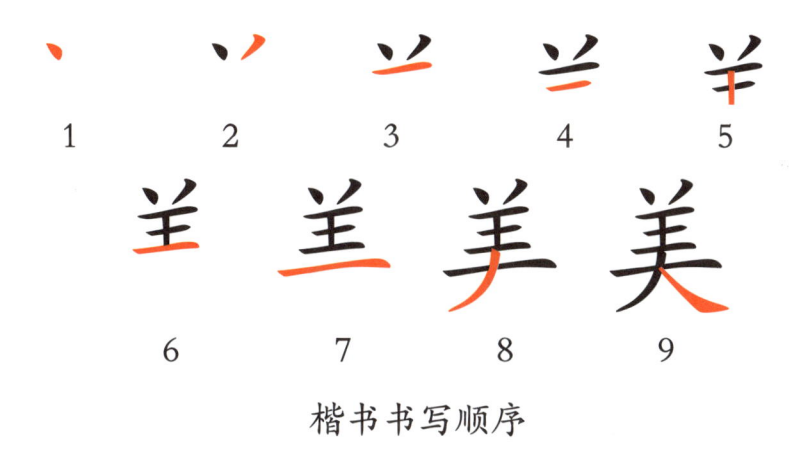

本义应指形貌容颜姣好。可引申为好、善、令人满意、鲜美等义。

The original meaning of the character "美" refers to a beautiful and attractive appearance. It can be extended to mean good, virtuous, satisfying, delicious, and other positive qualities.

美（甲骨文拓片）

与美组合的词有：美观、美术、美德、美景、美不胜收等。
Compound words related to the character "美" include:
1. 美观（měi guān）— Beautiful and pleasing to the eye
2. 美术（měi shù）— Fine arts
3. 美德（měi dé）— Virtue; Moral excellence
4. 美景（měi jǐng）— Beautiful scenery
5. 美不胜收（měi bù shèng shōu）— Too beautiful to be described

第六单元

yuè

乐

（其他读音：lè）

甲骨文"乐"字，从木，从二幺，像是木座上张开一丝弦之琴，以表示一种乐器琴瑟之形。后在"樂"字中间部位又加白声。"樂"为繁体字，今汉字简化规范写作"乐"为正体。属象形字。

The Oracle Bone Script character "乐" is composed of the radical "木"（wood）and the components "二幺"（representing strings or chords）. It depicts a musical instrument, possibly a stringed instrument like a zither or lyre, with strings stretched across a wooden frame. Later, in the character "樂", the addition of the component "白"（white）in the middle further represents sound or music. "樂" is a complex form, and in modern simplified Chinese characters, it is written as "乐" in standard form. This character belongs to the category of pictorial characters.

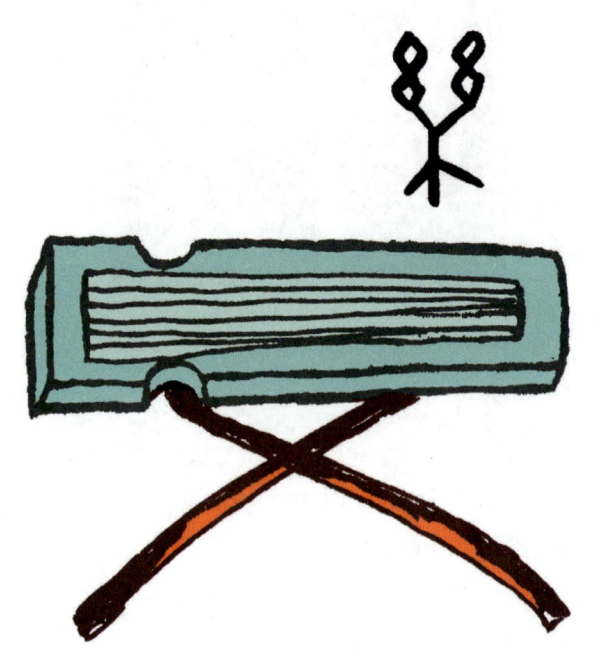

乐（示意图）

第六单元

一 ⺄ 乊 乐 乐
1　2　3　4　5

楷书书写顺序

本义是指乐器。可引申为音乐、快乐、安乐、可乐的事、喜好等义。

The original meaning of the character "乐" refers to musical instruments. It can be extended to mean music, joy, comfort, enjoyable things, preferences, and other related concepts.

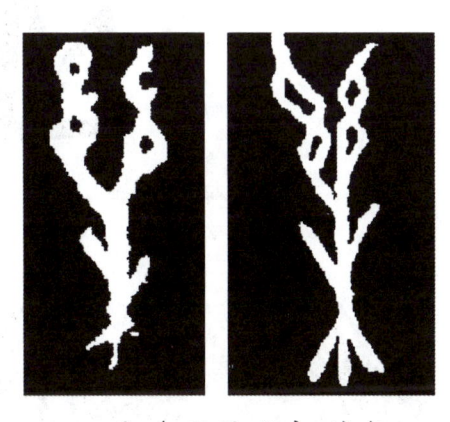

乐（甲骨文拓片）

与乐组合的词有：乐观、乐趣、乐此不疲等。

Compound words related to the character "乐" include:

1. 乐观（lè guān）– Optimistic
2. 乐趣（lè qù）– Pleasure; Delight
3. 乐此不疲（lè cǐ bù pí）– Delighted in it without getting tired

shān

山

甲骨文"山"字,像三个山头并列连绵起伏之形。属象形字。

The Oracle Bone Script character "山" is a pictorial character that depicts three mountain peaks arranged in a continuous, undulating way.

山(示意图)

第六单元

丨 山 山
  1   2   3
楷书书写顺序

本义指大山、山峰。可引申为像山一样的物体、蚕蔟、陵冢等义。

The original meaning of the character "山" refers to large mountains or mountain peaks. It can be extended to represent objects that resemble mountains, clusters of silkworms, burial mounds, and other related meanings.

山（甲骨文拓片）

与山组合的词有：山庄、山林、山清水秀、山盟海誓等。
Compound words related to the character "山" include:
1. 山庄（shān zhuāng）- Villa; Estate
2. 山林（shān lín）- Mountain forest
3. 山清水秀（shān qīng shuǐ xiù）- Beautiful mountains and clear waters
4. 山盟海誓（shān méng hǎi shì）- Vows of eteral love

第六单元

yì
易

甲骨文"易"字，像将一容器的酒倒入另一容器中之形，此可会更易之意。应为"锡"的本字。但易、锡表义有分工，锡从贝、易声，是易的加旁分化字。属会意字。

The Oracle Bone Script character "易" depicts the pouring of wine from one container into another, suggesting the concept of transferring or exchanging. This character likely originally represented the word "锡", meaning "to give" or "to bestow." However, the meanings of "易" and "锡" have diverged over time, with "锡" having the radical 贝（bèi）and "易" incorporating the sound component 易（yì）. In Oracle Bone Script, "易" is considered a compound ideogrammic character.

易（示意图）

第六单元

丨 冂 日 日 日 昜 易 易
1　2　3　4　5　6　7　8

楷书书写顺序

本义是指更易。可引申为改变、交换、容易、平坦、和悦、散漫、修治、敬辞等义。

The original meaning of "易" refers to exchange or transfer. It can be extended to mean change, swap, easy, smooth, harmonious, scattered, cultivate, polite language, etc.

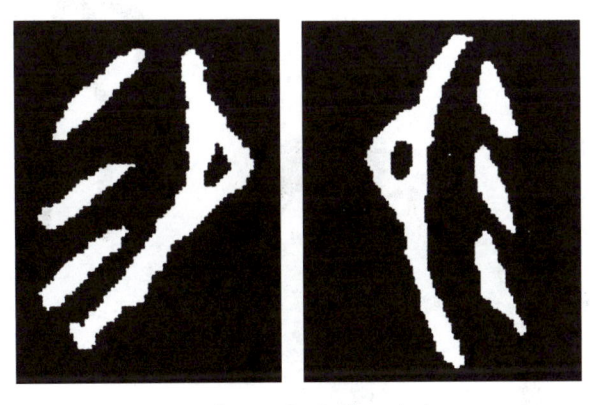

易（甲骨文拓片）

与易组合的词有：易碎、易地、易如反掌等。
Compound words related to the character "易" include:
1. 易碎（yì suì）– Fragile
2. 易地（yì dì）– Relocate
3. 易如反掌（yì rú fǎn zhǎng）– As easy as turning one's hand

第六单元

lǎo
老

甲骨文"老"字,像是一个长发扶杖老妇人的形象。古时老、考同源,字形皆是长发拄杖形,属象形字。

The Oracle Bone Script character "老" resembles the image of an elderly woman with long hair leaning on a walking stick. In ancient times, the characters for "老" and "考" shared the same origin, and their shapes both represented the image of an elderly person with long hair using a walking stick. This character belongs to the category of pictographic characters.

老(示意图)

第六单元

一 十 土 耂 耂 老
1　2　3　4　5　6

楷书书写顺序

本义是指老年人。可引申为历时长久、年岁大、不嫩、陈旧、有经验、死的讳称等义。

The original meaning of the Oracle Bone Script character "老" refers to an elderly person. It can be extended to mean lasting a long time, being of advanced age, not tender, old and outdated, having experience, and euphemisms for death, among other meanings.

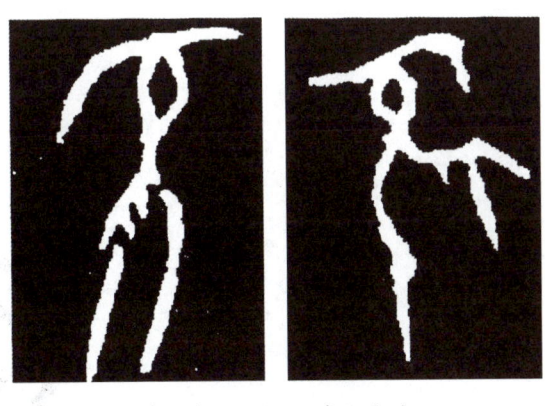

老（甲骨文拓片）

与老组合的词有：老师、老虎、老家、老老实实等。
Compound words related to the character "老" include:
1. 老师（lǎo shī）– Teacher
2. 老虎（lǎo hǔ）– Tiger
3. 老家（lǎo jiā）– Hometown
4. 老老实实（lǎo lǎo shí shí）– Honest and sincere

第六单元

shī

师

甲骨文"师",像两个连着的土堆形或小土丘之形。可会军队驻扎之意或代表军队。通"𠂤","師"为繁体字,今汉字简化规范写作"师"为正体。属象形字。

The Oracle Bone Script character "师" resembles two connected mounds of soil or small hillocks. It conveys the concept of a military encampment or represents an army. The traditional form of the character is "師", which is a more complex script, while the simplified form in modern Chinese is "师". This character belongs to the pictographic characters.

师(示意图)

第六单元

丨 丿 丿一 丿一 师 师
1　2　3　4　5　6

楷书书写顺序

本义指军队。可引申为众、都邑、教官、老师、技术之人、效法等义。

The original meaning of "师" refers to a military unit or army. It can be extended to mean a multitude, urban areas, military instructors, teachers, professionals, and the act of emulating or following.

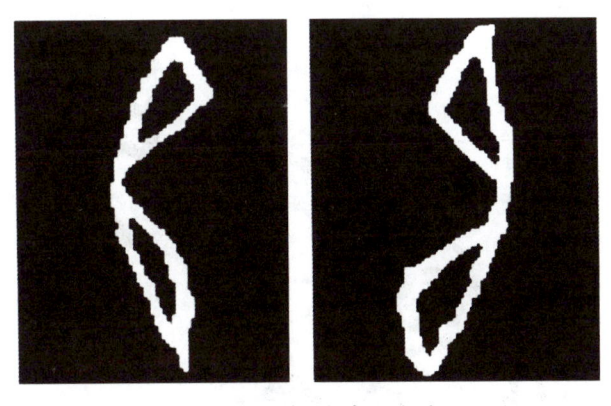

师（甲骨文拓片）

与师组合的词有：师傅、师生、师范大学、尊师重教等。

Compound words related to the character "师" include:

1. 师傅（shī fu）– Master; Skilled worker
2. 师生（shī shēng）– Teachers and students
3. 师范大学（shī fàn dà xué）– Normal university
4. 尊师重教（zūn shī zhòng jiào）– Respect the teacher and value education

第六单元

kě

可

甲骨文"可"字，从口，像口嘴之形；从丂，表示铁锄一类劳动工具之形，这里兼作标声。可会用歌以助劳之意。应为"歌"的初文。属形声会意字。

The Oracle Bone Script character "可" consists of a "口" (mouth) and "丂" (a symbol for a type of iron hoe or tool). This configuration resembles a mouth and signifies the sound of singing or chanting while using an iron hoe, suggesting the idea of using songs to assist in labor. It served as the primitive form for "歌", meaning song. It belongs to the category of pictophonetic characters.

可（示意图）

第六单元

一 亅 口 口 可

1　　2　　3　　4　　5

楷书书写顺序

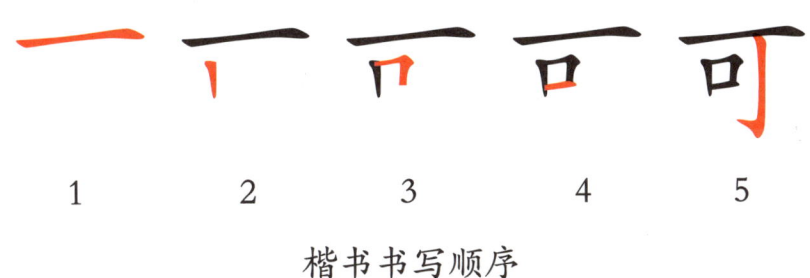

本义是指以歌助劳。引申为肯定、适合、对着、尽着、值得、能够、转折、意外许可、大约等义。

The original meaning is to use songs to aid labor. It is extended to imply affirmation, suitability, facing, yielding to, deserving, capable of, turning point, unexpected permission, approximately, and other meanings.

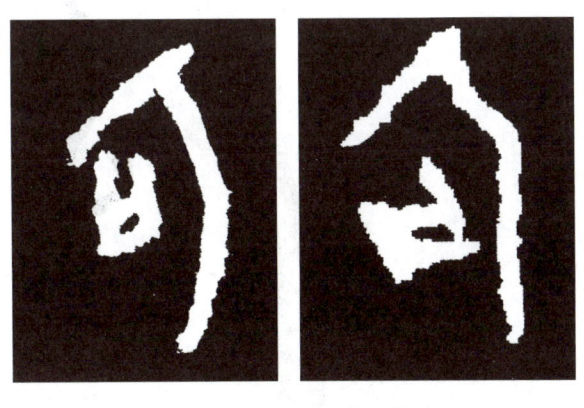

可（甲骨文拓片）

与可组合的词有：可以、可是、可靠、可能性等。
Compound words related to the character "可" include:
1. 可以（kě yǐ）– Can; May
2. 可是（kě shì）– But; However
3. 可靠（kě kào）– Reliable
4. 可能性（kě néng xìng）– Possibility

第六单元

yǐ

以

甲骨文"以"字，独体构型字，像古代翻地用的犁头、耖锸一类农具。属象形会意字。形同"厶"。假借作"私"。今汉字规范写作"以"为正体。

The character "以" in Oracle Bone Script is represented by a single, unique shape, resembling ancient farming tools such as a plow or a hoe. It belongs to the category of pictographic and ideographic characters, and it shares a similar form with the character "厶". It is borrowed to represent the meaning "private". In modern standardized Chinese writing, "以" is the accepted form.

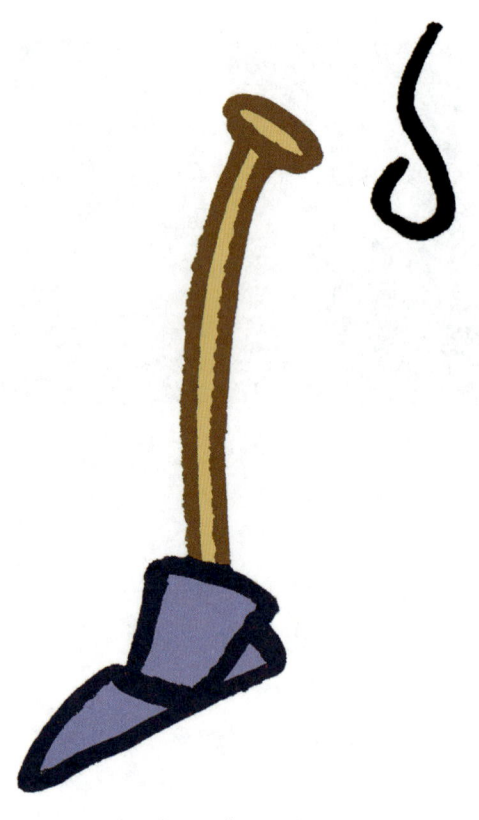

以（示意图）

第六单元

レ　レ　以　以
1　　2　　3　　4

楷书书写顺序

本义是指耒耜一类翻地犁头。可引申为原由、相似、用、为、在、依照等义。

The original meaning refers to farming tools used for turning the soil such as plowshares. It can be extended to mean reason, similarity, use, for, in, according to, etc.

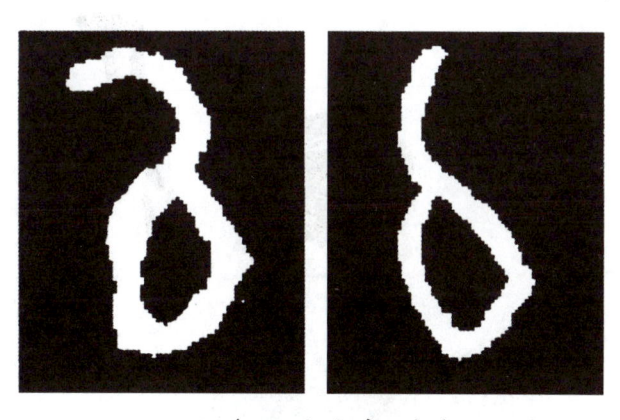

以（甲骨文拓片）

与以组合的词有：以后、以及、以前、以外、以理服人等。

Compound words related to the character "以" include:

1. 以后（yǐ hòu）– Later; Afterwards
2. 以及（yǐ jí）– As well as; And
3. 以前（yǐ qián）– Before; In the past
4. 以外（yǐ wài）– Outside; Beyond
5. 以理服人（yǐ lǐ fú rén）– To convince others by reasoning

第六单元

zhǎng

长

（其他读音：cháng）

甲骨文"长"字，像一长发老人之形，伛背且拄拐杖的老妇人，表示长者。又因头发之长，引申为长短之长。繁体字"長"，今汉字简化规范写作"长"为正体。

The Oracle Bone Script character "长" resembles the figure of an elderly woman with long hair, bent over and leaning on a walking stick, symbolizing an elderly person. It is also extended to represent the concept of length, both in terms of physical height and the length of hair. The traditional character "長" has been simplified to "长" in modern standardized Chinese.

长（示意图）

第六单元

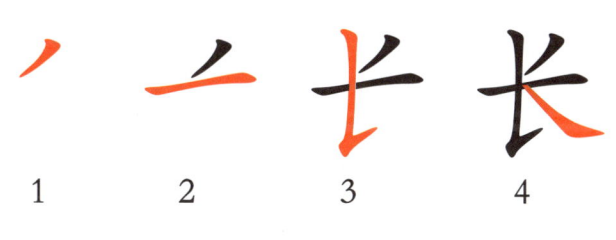

丿 一 长 长
1　2　3　4

楷书书写顺序

本义指年长，发长（因古人有不剪发之俗）。可引申为空间、长度、长处、擅长、岁数大、排行第一、辈分大、长官、生长、增加、多余等义。

The original meaning of "长" refers to being senior in age and having long hair（due to the ancient custom of not cutting hair）. It can be extended to denote concepts such as space, length, strengths, expertise, advanced age, ranking first, seniority, senior officer, growth, increase, surplus, and so on.

长（甲骨文拓片）

与长组合的词有：长期、长城、长久、长短、长方形、长辈、生长等。

Compound words related to the character "长" include:

1. 长期（cháng qī）– Long-term
2. 长城（cháng chéng）– The Great Wall
3. 长久（cháng jiǔ）– Long-lasting
4. 长短（cháng duǎn）– Length
5. 长方形（cháng fāng xíng）– Rectangle
6. 长辈（zhǎng bèi）– Elder
7. 生长（shēng zhǎng）– Growth

第六单元

zhě
者

甲骨文"者"字，从木，像古代燃烧木材之形，缀加点者表示溅出的火星，形同"燎"字。从口，像古时盛食物或蒸煮器皿之形，以"口"表示器皿之圆口。可会以木燃器皿之意。属会意字。

The Oracle Bone Script character "者" depicts the shape of burning wood in ancient times, with added dots to represent sparks splashing out, similar to the character "燎". It also includes the component "口", resembling the shape of a vessel used for containing or steaming food, with the "口" indicating the round opening of the vessel. This composition signifies the idea of using a wooden vessel for burning. It belongs to the category of ideogram and compound ideogram characters.

者（示意图）

第六单元

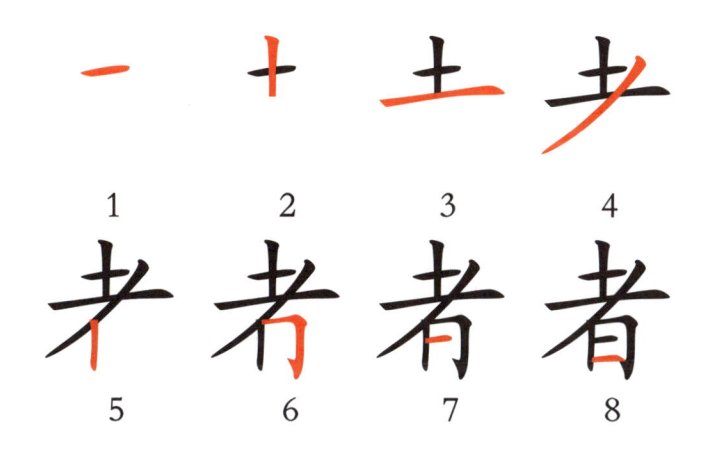

一 十 土 耂
1　2　3　4

耂 者 者 者
5　6　7　8

楷书书写顺序

本义为燃煮器皿。可引申为指称人或事物、语气助词、表示假设、犹这、应诺声等义。

The original meaning is to burn or cook in a vessel. It can be extended to refer to people or things, serve as a modal particle, express assumptions, similar to "this" or affirmative responses, etc.

者（甲骨文拓片）

与者组合的词有：来者、作者、勇者无畏等。

Compound words related to the character "者" include:

1. 来者（lái zhě）– The one who comes; Newcomers
2. 作者（zuò zhě）– Author
3. 勇者无畏（yǒng zhě wú wèi）– The brave are fearless

121

cóng

从

甲骨文"从"字为左右结构,像两个面朝同一方向的人,前后相从。会相跟随之意。"從"为繁体字,今汉字简化规范写作"从"为正体。属会意字。

The Oracle Bone Script for the character "从" features a left-right structure resembling two people facing the same direction, indicating following one another. The character implies the idea of accompanying or following. The variant "從" is the complex form, while the modern simplified form is written as "从". It belongs to the category of ideogrammic compounds.

从(示意图)

第七单元

丿 人 从 从
1　2　3　4

楷书书写顺序

本义是指相从而行。可引申为顺从、参与、采用、追随、加入、从属、次要的等义。

The original meaning refers to walking or moving together in accordance. It can be extended to signify compliance, participation, adoption, following, joining, subordination, secondary, and so on.

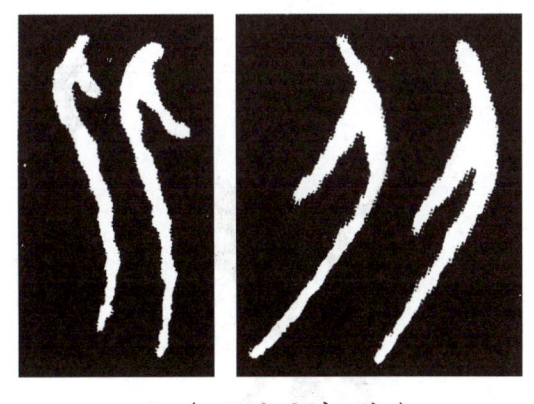

从（甲骨文拓片）

与从组合的词有：从事、从而、从前、从头做起等。
Compound words related to the character "从" include:
1. 从事（cóng shì）– Engage in
2. 从而（cóng ér）– Thus; Thereby
3. 从前（cóng qián）– Formerly
4. 从头做起（cóng tóu zuò qǐ）– Start from scratch

第七单元

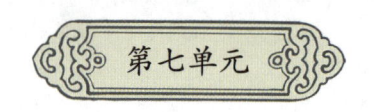

甲骨文"事"字,上方像是狩猎工具猎叉之形,下从又,像手之形。表示手持捕猎工具去田猎做事之意。属会意字。通假"使","吏"字。

The Oracle Bone Script character "事" depicts an upper part resembling the shape of a hunting fork, and below it is the component "又", resembling the shape of a hand. This composition signifies the idea of using a hand to hold a hunting to and engage in hunting or work in the fields. It belongs to the category of ideogram and compound ideogram characters. It is interchangeable with characters such as "使"（shǐ）and "吏"（lì）.

shì

事

（通"使、吏"）

事（示意图）

第七单元

楷书书写顺序

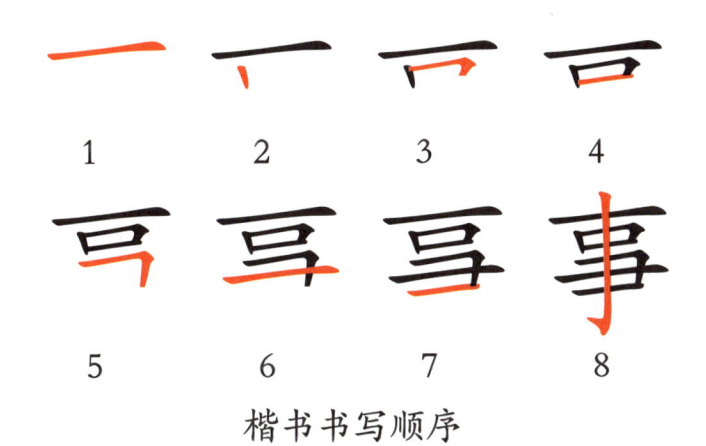

本义指田猎做事。引申为为王记事之人、事物发展之进程、从事、战事、侍奉、事件、事故等义。

The original meaning refers to hunting or working in the fields. It is extended to signify a person who records events for the king, the development process of things, as well as engaging in activities, military affairs, serving, events, accidents, etc.

事（甲骨文拓片）

与事组合的词有：事情、事业、事物、事必躬亲等。
Compound words related to the character "事" include:
1. 事情（shì qing）– Thing; Matter
2. 事业（shì yè）– Career; Undertaking
3. 事物（shì wù）– Thing; Object
4. 事必躬亲（shì bì gōng qīn）– One must personally attend to a task

第七单元

shí

时

甲骨文"时"字,下方从日,像太阳形;上方从之,表示脚趾自起点向前走之形,此兼表声。会时序之意。属会意字。"時"为繁体字,今汉字简化规范写作"时"为正体。

The Oracle Bone Script character "时" features the component "日" below, resembling the shape of the sun. Above it is another component which not only represents the form of toes walking forward from the starting point, but also indicate the sound. This composition signifies the idea of the sequence of time. The complex form is "時", while the modern simplified form is written as "时" in regular script. It belongs to the category of ideogram and compound ideogram characters.

时(示意图)

126

第七单元

丨 冂 冂 日 日 时 时
1　2　3　4　5　6　7

楷书书写顺序

本义指时序。可引申为时间、时辰、计时单位等义。

The original meaning refers to the sequence of time. It is extended to signify time, hour, and units of measurement for time.

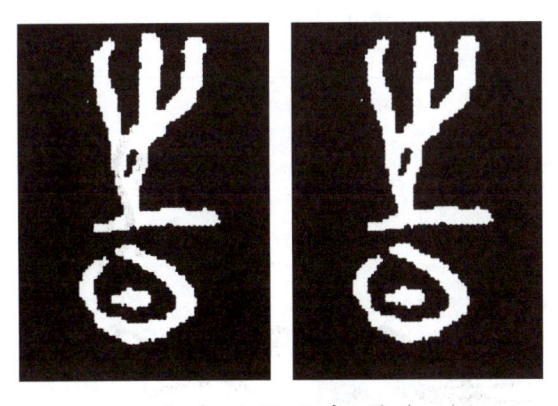

时（甲骨文拓片）

与时组合的词有：时代、时期、时尚、时间表等。
Compound words related to the character "时" include:
1. 时代（shí dài）– Era
2. 时期（shí qī）– Period
3. 时尚（shí shàng）– Fashion
4. 时间表（shí jiān biǎo）– Schedule; Timetable

第七单元

jiāng

江

甲骨文"江"字左边从水,中间长曲画下端带有贯穿的箭头,像穿越山崖之意。两侧点画表示江河水流或飞溅的水滴。右从工字部为形声符。属形声字。

The Oracle Bone Script character "江" is a pictophonetic character. On the left side is the component "水", representing water. In the middle, there is a long and curved stroke with a pointed arrowhead at the bottom, resembling the idea of traversing or piercing through a mountain cliff. The dots on both sides represent the flowing or splashing water droplets of rivers and streams. On the right side is the component "工", serving as a pictophonetic element.

江(示意图)

第七单元

丶 氵 氵 汀 汀 江
1　2　3　4　5　6

楷书书写顺序

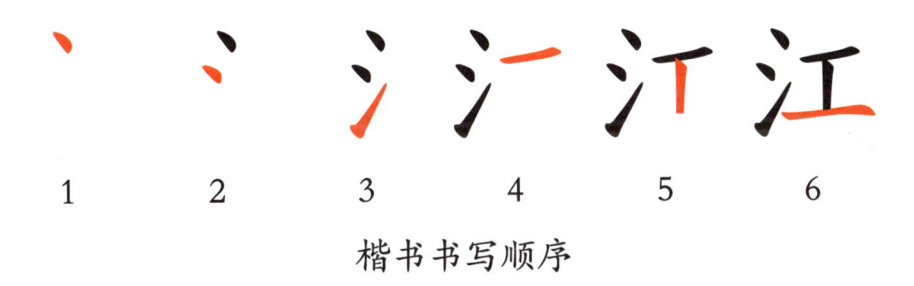

本义为长江，中国境内第一大河。后来词义范围扩大，引申成为大河流的通称。

The original meaning of "江" refers to the Yangtze River, the largest river in China. Over time, the semantic range expanded, and it became a generic term for large rivers.

江（甲骨文拓片）

与江组合的词有：江湖、江轮、江山如画等。
Compound words related to the character "江" include:
1. 江湖（jiāng hú）– Rivers and lakes, The world
2. 江轮（jiāng lún）– Riverboat; Paddle steamer
3. 江山如画（jiāng shān rú huà）– Scenic rivers and mountains; Picturesque landscape

第七单元

hé
河

甲骨文"河"字,从水,像水流之形。从何、从丂或水旁之旁从一曲线、省点等形式,在这里皆作标声。表示河流之意。属形声字。

The Oracle Bone Script character "河" is a pictophonetic character. The component on the left is "水", representing water and resembling the flow of water. The components on the right include "何","丂", or a curved line near the water radical, all serving as phonetic elements. In this context, they act as sound indicators. The character as a whole signifies the concept of a river.

河(示意图)

第七单元

丶 氵 氵 氵
1　2　3　4

氵 氵 河 河
5　6　7　8

楷书书写顺序

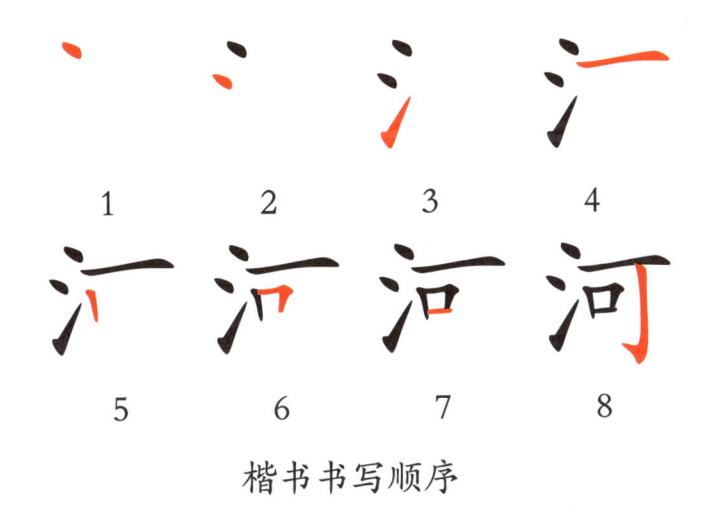

本义是指河。可引申为水名、地名、银河等义。

The original meaning of the Oracle Bone Script character "河" refers to the river. It can be extended to names of rivers, places, the Milky Way, etc.

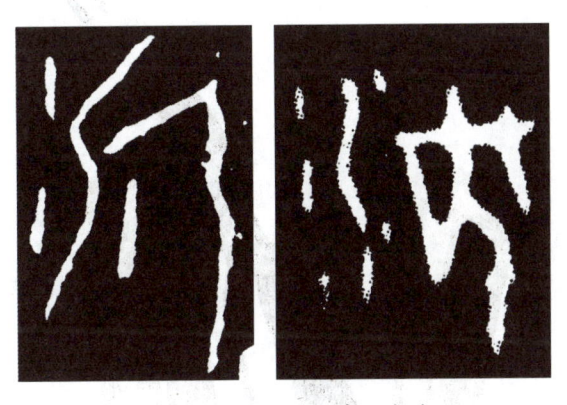

河（甲骨文拓片）

与河组合的词有：河道、河山、河床、亚马孙河等。
Compound words related to the character "河" include:
1. 河道（hé dào）– River channel
2. 河山（hé shān）– Rivers and mountains; Landscapes
3. 河床（hé chuáng）– Riverbed
4. 亚马孙河（yà mǎ sūn hé）– The Amazon River

第七单元

fēn

分

甲骨文"分"字,外面是个"八"字,中间是一把刀,表示用刀劈开木材或物体的形状。此会以刀分物之意。属会意字。

The Oracle Bone Script character " 分 " consists of the outer part resembling the shape of the number "八" （eight） and the middle part representing a knife. This composition signifies the action of using a knife to split or divide wood or other objects. This character belongs to the category of ideogram and compound ideogram characters, specifically conveying the idea of cutting or dividing things with a knife.

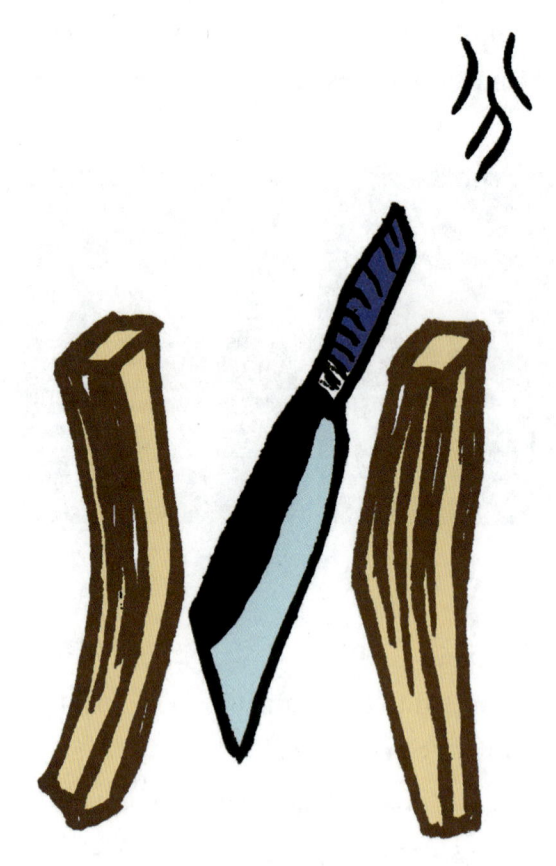

分（示意图）

第七单元

丿 八 分 分
1　2　3　4

楷书书写顺序

本义是指分割，或分开。可引申为辨别、一半、四季昼夜之分、各种单位、成分、分支、离散、分配等义。

The original meaning refers to cutting, dividing, or separating. It can be extended to signify distinguishing, half, the division of the four seasons and day and night, various units, components, branches, dispersion, distribution, etc.

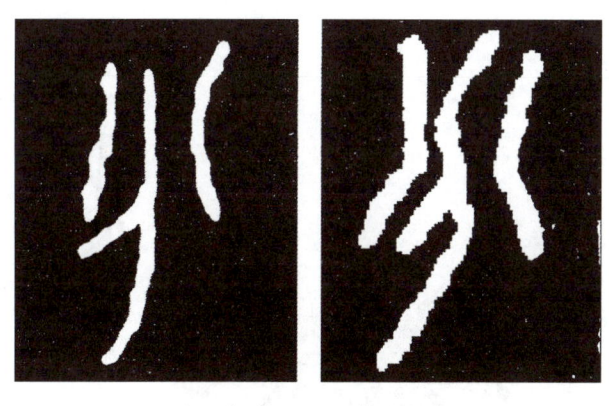

分（甲骨文拓片）

与分组合的词有：分布、分配、分辨、分寸、分秒必争等。
Compound words related to the character "分" include:
1. 分布（fēn bù）– Distribution
3. 分配（fēn pèi）– Allocation; Distribution
4. 分辨（fēn biàn）– Distinguish; Differentiate
5. 分寸（fēn cun）– Sense of propriety; Moderation
6. 分秒必争（fēn miǎo bì zhēng）– Every second counts; Time is of the essence

第七单元

nián

年

甲骨文"年"字,异体写作"秂",上从禾,下从人,两形会意,表示人背负着成熟的谷物,会丰收之年意。庄稼一年一熟,庄稼收获了,一年过去了。属会意字。

The Oracle Bone Script character "年" is a compound ideogram. It has an alternative form written as "秂". The upper part is the component "禾", representing grains or crops, and the lower part is "人", representing a person. The combination of the two components signifies a person carrying mature grains, symbolizing a year of abundant harvest. As crops get ripe once a year, the character reflects the concept of the passing of a year after the harvest.

年(示意图)

第七单元

丿 ㇒ 𠂉 午 年 年
1　2　3　4　5　6

楷书书写顺序

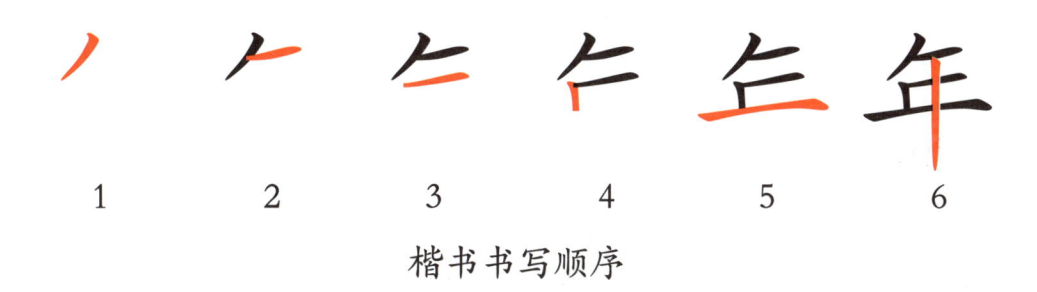

本义指人负禾、谷物成熟。引申为一年收成、过年、岁月、时光、年龄、寿命、时间单位等。

The original meaning refers to a person carrying ripe grains or crops. It is extended to signify a year of harvest, celebrating the New Year, years and months, time, age, lifespan, and units of time.

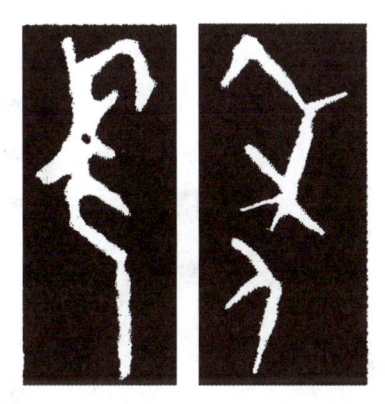

年（甲骨文拓片）

与年组合的词有：年代、年轻、年级等。
Compound words related to the character "年" include:
1. 年代（nián dài）– Era; Age
2. 年轻（nián qīng）– Young
3. 年级（nián jí）– Grade; Year in school

第七单元

jīn
今

甲骨文"今"字，上方从∧，像一个口向下的器物盖子之形（甲骨文"会""食""合"等字上方之∧皆为盖意）。下从一，像一小器物。两形会意，表示用盖子盖住小器物之意。属会意字。

The Oracle Bone Script character "今" features the component "∧" above, resembling the shape of a container lid or cover facing downward.（In Oracle Bone Script characters like "会", "食", "合", etc, the "∧" component above signifies a lid or cover.）Below is the component "—", resembling a small object. The combination of the two components signifies the act of covering a small object with a lid, indicating the meaning of "now" or "today". The character belongs to the category of ideogram and compound ideogram characters.

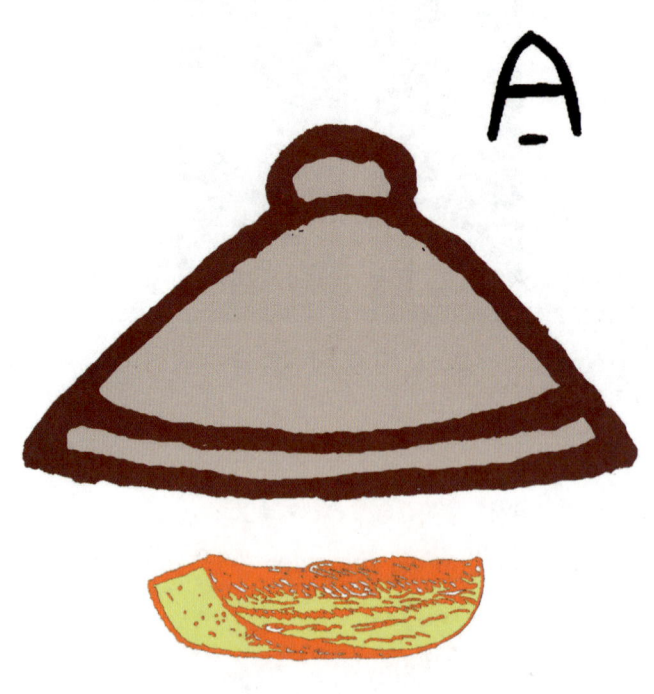

今（示意图）

136

第七单元

丿 人 仒 今
1　2　3　4

楷书书写顺序

本义指把物体盖住。可引申为现在、现代、即将、假如等义。

The original meaning refers to covering an object with a lid. It can be extended to signify the present, modern times, imminent actions, assumptions, and so on.

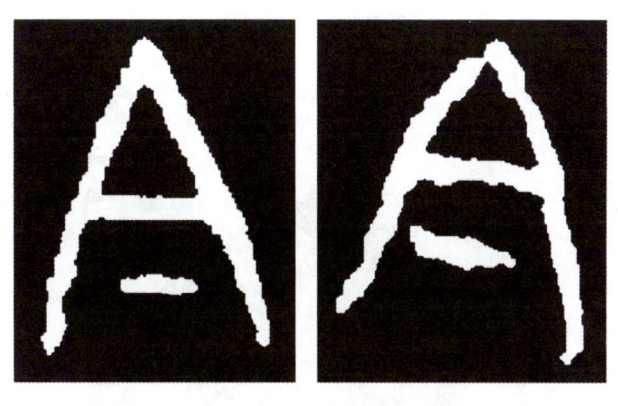

今（甲骨文拓片）

与今组合的词有：今年、今晚、今非昔比等。

Compound words related to the character "今" include:

1. 今年（jīn nián）– This year
2. 今晚（jīn wǎn）– Tonight
3. 今非昔比（jīn fēi xī bǐ）– Not comparable to the past; Incomparable

第七单元

甲骨文"图"字，像仓形，从口，像器物口形。此可会有器物存放仓内之意。啚即为"图"，并通"鄙"字。属会意字。

The Oracle Bone Script character "图" resembles the shape of a storage vessel or warehouse, with the component "口" indicating the shape of the opening of the container. This composition suggests the idea of storing objects within a warehouse. The character "啚"is an ancient variant of "图" and is also interchangeable with the character "鄙". Both characters belong to the category of ideogram and compound ideogram characters, specifically conveying the concept of storing or depicting.

tú

图

图（示意图）

第七单元

丨冂冂㐭㐭㐭㐭图
1　2　3　4　5　6　7　8
楷书书写顺序

本义为藏谷之仓。可引申为边邑、小邑、构想、粗陋、识浅、计谋、图形等义。

The original meaning refers to a granary or warehouse for storing grains. It can be extended to signify border towns, small towns, ideas, simplicity, shallowness, strategies, diagrams, etc.

图（甲骨文拓片）

与图组合的词有：画图、图像、图书、图形、地图等。
Compound words related to the character"图"include:
1. 画图（huà tú）– Drawing; Sketching
2. 图像（tú xiàng）– Image
3. 图书（tú shū）– Books
4. 图形（tú xíng）– Graphics; Figure
5. 地图（dì tú）– Map

139

第七单元

guǎn
馆

　　甲骨文"馆"即"官"字，上方宝盖头表示房屋，特指官府。下方部首即表示山丘。会建屋于阜之意，此是旅途中止息之官舍，故"官"为"馆"之初文。也作驻军的营地。官指地而非指人。属会意字。

　　The Oracle Bone Script character "馆", equivalent to the modern character "官", depicts a structure with a roof on top, representing a building, specifically an official residence or government office. The component below symbolizes a hill, indicating construction on a hill. This combination suggests building houses on a hill, specifically referring to an official rest stop during a journey. Therefore, it is the earliest form of the character "馆", which later also refers to a military camp. In this context, "官" refers to a location rather than a person. This character belongs to the category of ideogram and compound ideogram characters.

馆（示意图）

第七单元

1 2 3 4 5 6 7 8 9 10 11

楷书书写顺序

本义是官府，房舍、屋殿。可引申为客馆、官署、官职等义。

The original meaning refers to an official residence, government office, or a building. It can be extended to refer to a guesthouse, administrative office, official position, and so on.

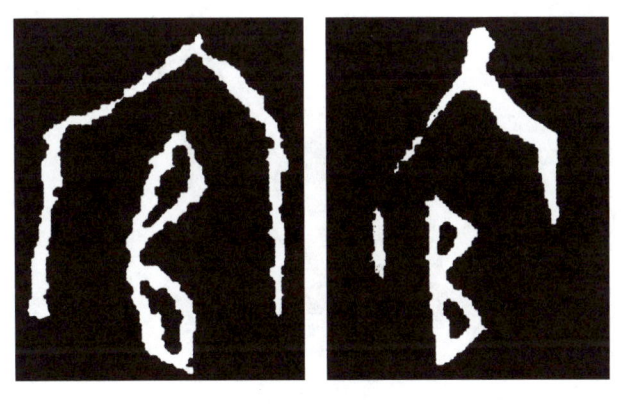

馆（甲骨文拓片）

与馆组合的词有：旅馆、博物馆、图书馆、照相馆等。
Compound words related to the character "馆" include:
1. 旅馆（lǚ guǎn）— Inn; Hotel
2. 博物馆（bó wù guǎn）— Museum
3. 图书馆（yóu yǒng guǎn）— Library
4. 照相馆（zhào xiàng guǎn）— Photography studio

第八单元

liǎo

了

（其他读音：le）

　　甲骨文"了"字，从子，上方像小孩头上长有毛发，此为从子的特征。下像小孩不见臂、足的样子。凡物二股或一股结纠缭缚不直伸者，曰了戾。而了字从子，正是四肢被裹在襁褓中之状。属象形会意字。

　　The Oracle Bone Script character "了" features the component "子"（child）, with the upper part resembling the hair on a child's head, a distinctive feature of "子". The lower part depicts a child without visible arms or legs. It represents objects with two or one tangled or bound strands, not extending straight, referred to "了戾". The character "了" from "子" precisely illustrates the state of four limbs wrapped in swaddling clothes. It belongs to the category of pictophonetic compound characters.

了（示意图）

第八单元

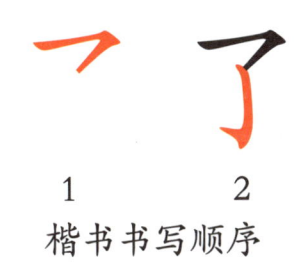

了 了
1　2
楷书书写顺序

　　本义指不见臂足的孩童。引申为全然、结束、清楚的、明白的或使用作为语气助词等义，或作助词，表示动作完成的时态，读 le。

The original meaning refers to a child without visible arms and legs. It is extended to signify entirety, completion, clarily, understanding, or used as a modal particle to imply the completion of an action, etc.

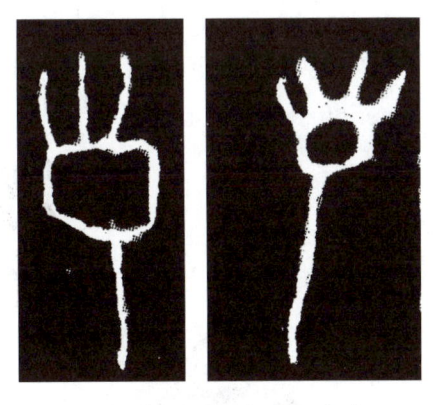

了（甲骨文拓片）

　　与了组合的词有：了解、了不起、了却心愿、了如指掌、好了等。
Compound words related to the character"了"include:

1. 了解（liǎo jiě）– To understand
2. 了不起（liǎo bu qǐ）– Remarkable; Fantastic
3. 了却心愿（liǎo què xīn yuàn）– To fulfill a wish
4. 了如指掌（liǎo rú zhǐ zhǎng）– To know something inside out
5. 好了（hǎ le）– Done

第八单元

guò

过

甲骨文"过"字,从彳,像行道路口之形;从戈,本像古代长柄戈戟兵器,这里作标声;从止,像脚趾之形。表示有人在路上走过之意。属形声字。"過"为繁体字,今汉字简化规范写作"过"为正体。

The Oracle Bone Script character "过" depicts a composition of three components. The first component, "彳" (chì), resembles the form of crossroads or intersection of paths. The second component, "戈" (gē), originally symbolizing ancient long-handled weapons like spears and halberds, serves here as a phonetic component indicating the sound. The third component, "止" (zhǐ), takes the shape of toes, representing the concept of stopping or walking. Together, these elements convey the meaning of someone walking on the road or crossing a path. This character "过" falls into the category of pictophonetic characters. "過" is the traditional script, and in modern simplified Chinese writing, "过" is used in standard form.

过(示意图)

第八单元

一 丁 寸 寸 讨 过
1　2　3　4　5　6

楷书书写顺序

本义是经过、行走过。引申为拜访、探望、度过（某段时间）、超越、胜过、失误、过错（与"功"相对）等义。或作助词，用在表示动作的词后面，表示行为完毕或曾经发生。

The original meaning of the character "过" is to pass through or walk across. It is extended to signify visiting, paying respects, spend some time, surpassing, making mistakes, used as a modal particle after a verb to imply the completion of an action or something has taken place, and other meanings.

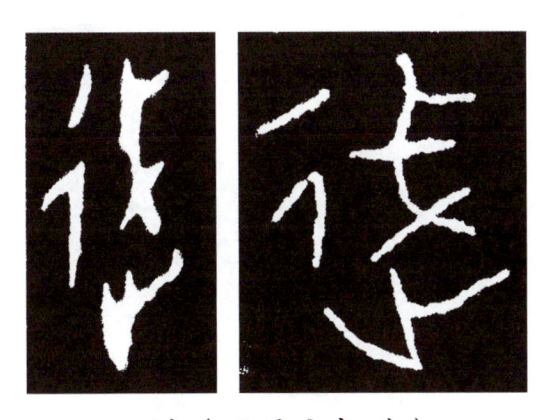

过（甲骨文拓片）

与过组合的词有：过程、过去、过年、过目不忘等。
Compound words related to the character "过" include:
1. 过程（guò chéng）– Process
2. 过去（guò qù）– The past
3. 过年（guò nián）– Celebrate the New Year
4. 过目不忘（guò mù bù wàng）– Photographic memory

第八单元

hui

回

甲骨文"回"字,像流水回旋的形狀,为了便于用刀镌刻,水流的圆曲之笔改成了直笔。属象形字。

The Oracle Bone Script character "回" is a pictographic character, depicting the shape of water flowing and swirling. For convenience of carving with a knife, the curved strokes representing the circular flow of water were modified into straight strokes.

回(示意图)

第八单元

丨 冂 冂 冋 冋 回
1 2 3 4 5 6

楷书书写顺序

本义为水流旋转、回旋。引申为改变方向掉转、返回、回头、回复、曲折等义。也作量词，用于行为、事件等，或用于章回小说、评书等，相当于"章"。

The original meaning of the character "回" is the rotation and swirling of water flow. It is extended to signify changing direction, turning around, returning, replying, winding, being intricate, or be used as a measure word, used in an action or event, or used in chapter-styled novels or storytelling which is equivalent to the word chapter, among other meanings.

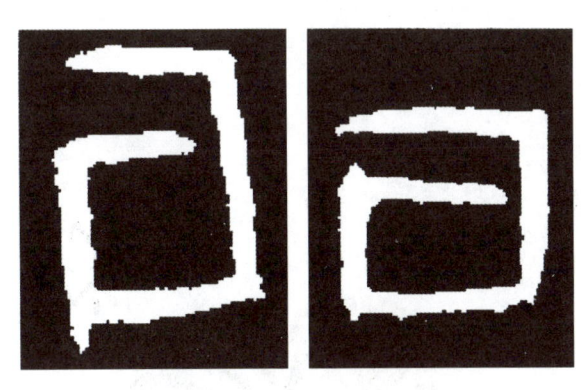

回（甲骨文拓片）

与回组合的词有：回答、回家、回忆、回报、回心转意等。
Compound words related to the character "回" include:

1. 回答（huí dá）– Answer
2. 回家（huí jiā）– Go home
3. 回忆（huí yì）– Recall; Memories
4. 回报（huí bào）– Repay; Return
5. 回心转意（huí xīn zhuǎn yì）– Change one's mind; Have a change of heart

第八单元

lái

来

甲骨文"来"是"麥"的本字,像是一棵成熟了的小麦形。上部是麦穗,中间两侧是麦叶,下端是麦根。"來"为繁体字,今汉字简化规范写作"来"为正体。属象形字。"来"与"禾"字易混淆,其主要区别在:"来"字斜画上端下弯,禾字斜画上端无弯钩。

The Oracle Bone Script character "来", which is the original word of "麥", resembles a mature wheat plant. The upper part represents the wheat ears, with wheat leaves on both sides in the middle, and the wheat roots at the bottom. "來" is the traditional script, and in modern simplified Chinese writing, "来" is used in standard form. It belongs to the category of pictograms. The main distinction between "来" and the character for "wheat"(禾) is that in "来", the diagonal stroke at the upper end bends downward, while the character for "禾" lacks this downward bend in the diagonal stroke at the upper end.

来(示意图)

第八单元

一 丆 乛 业 来 来 来

1　2　3　4　5　6　7

楷书书写顺序

本义为小麦。本义消失，后引申为从别处到这里（跟"去"相对）、（情况、事情等）出现、发生、将来的、趋向、约数、未来、向往的等义。

The original meaning of the character "来" is wheat. When its original meaning disappeared, it was extended to signify arrival (the opposite of "go"), future, tendency, approximate number, the future, and longing for.

来（甲骨文拓片）

与来组合的词有：来信、来访、来历、来得及、来之不易等。

Compound words related to the character "来" include:

1. 来信（lái xìn）– Incoming letter
2. 来访（lái fǎng）– Visit
3. 来历（lái lì）– Origin; History
4. 来得及（lái de jí）– There's still time; Be able to make it
5. 来之不易（lái zhī bù yì）– Hard-won; Not easy to come by

第八单元

huì

会

甲骨文"会"字，上从亼，像食盖之形。中间从口或从日，表示古代做饭、盛食用的炊具。下从口，表示烧火加热的器皿之形。三形会意即表示会合之义。"會"为繁体字，今汉字简化规范写作"会"为正体。属会意字。

The Oracle Bone Script character "会" is composed of three elements. The first element, "亼", resembles the shape of a food cover. The second element is either "口" or "日", indicating ancient cooking or food containers. The third element, "口", depicts the form of a vessel used for heating or cooking over a fire. The combination of these three elements signifies the concept of gathering or meeting. "會" is the trditional script, and in modern simplified Chinese writing, "会"is used in standard form, and it belongs to the category of ideogrammic compound characters.

会（示意图）

第八单元

丿 人 人 亽 会 会
1　2　3　4　5　6

楷书书写顺序

　　本义是指会合。可引申为聚会、遇见、理解、熟悉、庙会、学会、应当、时机、恰巧等义。

The original meaning of the character "会" is to gather or meet. It can be extended to signify gathering, encountering, understanding, being familiar with, temple fair, learning, should, timing, and happening to, among other meanings.

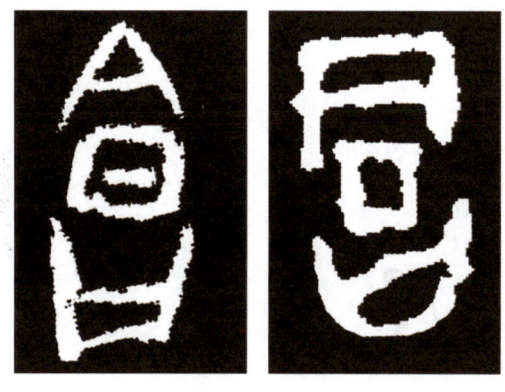

会（甲骨文拓片）

　　与会组合的词有：会议、会堂、会员证、会心一笑等。

Compound words related to the character "会" include:

1. 会议（huì yì）– Meeting; conference
2. 会堂（huì táng）– Assembly hall
3. 会员证（huì yuán zhèng）– Membership card
4. 会心一笑（huì xīn yī xiào）– A knowing smile; A smile of understanding

第八单元

qián

前

甲骨文"前"字，上方从止，表示足迹，下方从舟，表示人坐在船上，不用脚走也不用划水，舟随水流自然向前，两侧增有行道符号表示沿一定道路向前。属会意字。

The Oracle Bone Script character "前" is a compound ideogram. The upper part features the character "止" (stop), representing footprints. The lower part is the pictograph for a boat. In the Oracle Bone Script, "前" depicts a person sitting in a boat, not walking with their feet or rowing. The boat naturally moves forward with the flow of water, and symbols on both sides indicate moving forward along a specific path.

前（示意图）

第八单元

丶 丷 䒑 䒑 䒑
1　2　3　4　5

䒑 䒑 前 前
6　7　8　9

楷书书写顺序

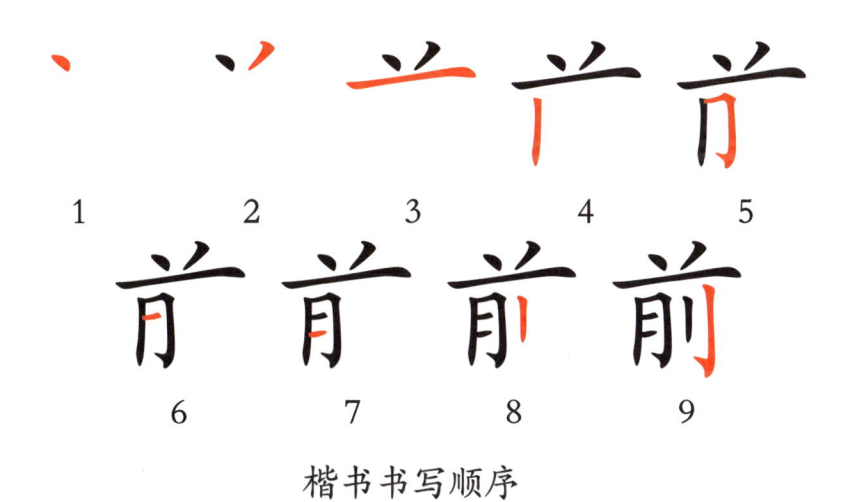

本义指不行而进。引申为前面、从前、空间、时间、行进等义。

The original meaning of the character "前" is to move forward without walking. It is extended to signify the front, the past, space, time, and progression, among other meanings.

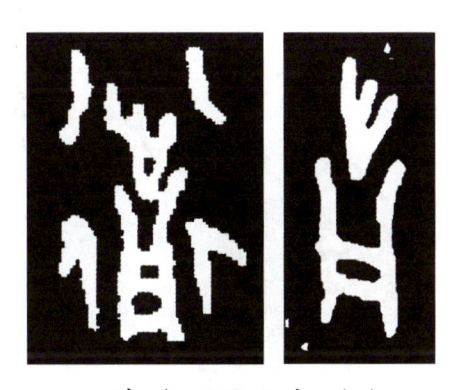

前（甲骨文拓片）

与前组合的词有：前进、前景、前奏曲、前途无量等。
Compound words related to the character "前" include:
1. 前进（qián jìn）– Advance; Move forward
2. 前景（qián jǐng）– Prospect; Outlook
3. 前奏曲（qián zòu qǔ）– Prelude
4. 前途无量（qián tú wú liàng）– Boundless prospects

第八单元

hòu

后

甲骨文"后",上方像一束丝的符号,表示绳索。下面是一个倒止符号,表示向后的脚迹。两形会意表示脚被绳索系住,行动不能向前而落于后边之意。"後"为繁体字,今汉字简化规范写作"后"为正体字。属会意字。

The Oracle Bone Script character "后" is a compound ideogram. The upper part resembles a symbol for "silk", representing a rope. Below is an inverted "止" symbol, indicating footprints moving backward. This signifies that the feet are bounded by a rope, preventing forward movement and implying a backward direction. "後" is the traditional script and in modern simplified Chinese, "后" is used as the standard form.

后(示意图)

第八单元

一 厂 厂 斤 斤 后 后
1　2　3　4　5　6

楷书书写顺序

本义指落在后边、与"前"相反。引申为专指背面的事物，排序、时间较晚的以及后代等义。值得说明的是，这里的"后（後）"只是指前后之后的意义与范畴，它与另一个"后"（帝后的"后"）的用法与意义是不同的。

The original meaning of the character "后" is to fall behind, opposite to the front. It is extended to specifically refer to things on the backside, later in order or time, and descendants. It's important to note that in this context, "后（後）" only refers to the concept of being behind or later in a sequence, and its usage and meaning are different from the other "后" (referring to the empress or queen consort).

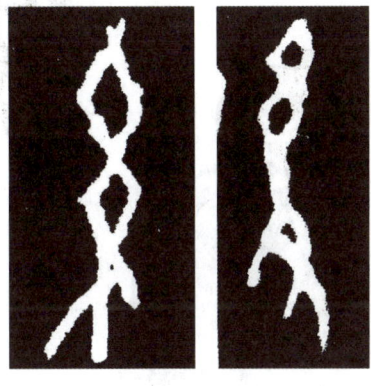

后（甲骨文拓片）

与后组合的词有：后退、后代、后起之秀等。
Compound words related to the character "后" include:

1. 后退（hòu tuì）– Retreat; Move backward
2. 后代（hòu dài）– Descendants; Later generations
3. 后起之秀（hòu qǐ zhī xiù）– Rising star; Young talent

155

第八单元

shuō

说

甲骨文"说"字即为"兑"字，通"悦""阅""锐"从人，像人侧立之形。从口，像人嘴巴形。从八，表示分开。此可会人咧嘴嬉笑，心情喜悦之意。属会意字。

The Oracle Bone Script character "说" is the same as the character "兑". It is composed of the component "人"（person）, resembling the shape of a person standing sideways. Below it is "口"（mouth）, resembling the shape of a person's mouth. The addition of "八"（eight）signifies separation. This composition conveys the meaning of a person grinning or smiling happily, indicating a joyful mood. It belongs to the category of ideogrammatic characters.

说（示意图）

第八单元

讠 讠 讠 讠 讠
1　2　3　4　5

讠 讠 讠 说
6　7　8　9

楷书书写顺序

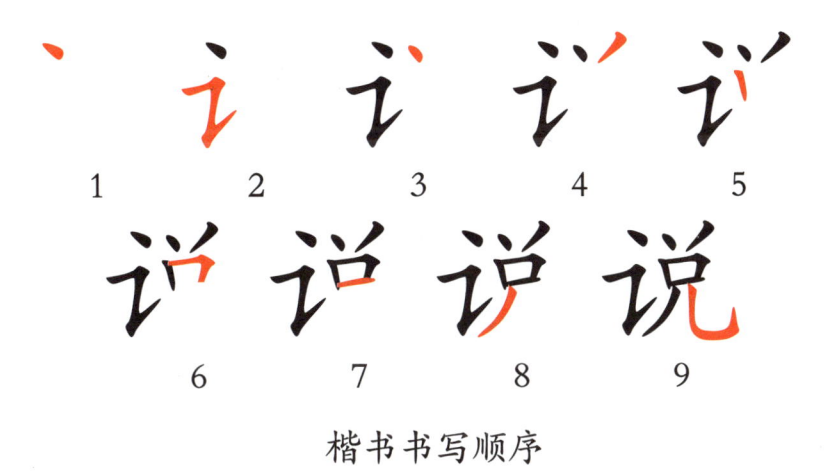

本义是指喜悦开心。可引申为言论、责备、说合、介绍等义。

The original meaning of the character "说" is to express joy and happiness. It can be extended to signify speech, criticism, persuasion, introduction, and other meanings.

说（甲骨文拓片）

与说组合的词有：说明、说话、说服、说到做到等。
Compound words related to the character "说" include:
1. 说明（shuō míng）– Explanation; Explain
2. 说话（shuō huà）– Speak; Talk
3. 说服（shuō fú）– Persuade; Convince
4. 说到做到（shuō dào zuò dào）– Practice what one preaches

yīn

因

甲骨文"因"为"茵"的本字,从口,像方席之形。口中大字部系"夂"之伪,乃为茵席编织之纹。属象形字。

The Oracle Bone Script character "因", which is the original word of "茵," is composed of the component "口", resembling the shape of a square mat or cushion. Inside "口" is the character "大", connected to a pseudo character "夂". This forms the pattern of weaving a cushion, indicating the initial meaning of "因" as a cushion. It belongs to the category of pictographic characters.

因(示意图)

第八单元

丨 冂 冃 因 因 因
1　2　3　4　5　6

楷书书写顺序

　　本义是指席子，可引申为原因（跟"果"相对）、凭借、根据、沿袭、因缘、因为等义。

The original meaning of the character "因" is a cushion or mat. It can be extended to signify reliance, basis, inheritance, reason (copposite to "consequence"), causality, because, among other meanings.

因（甲骨文拓片）

　　与因组合的词有：因为、因此、因素、因果、因材施教等。
Compound words related to the character "因" include:
1. 因为（yīn wèi）– Because
2. 因此（yīn cǐ）– Therefore
3. 因素（yīn sù）– Factor
4. 因果（yīn guǒ）– Cause and effect
5. 因材施教（yīn cái shī jiào）– Teach according to individual aptitude

第八单元

wèi

为

（其他读音：wéi）

甲骨文"为"是"爲"的本字，从又从象，像一个人用手控制大象的鼻形，役使其为人类劳动干活，即役象之意。"為""爲"为繁体字，今汉字简化规范写作"为"为正体。属象形会意字。

The Oracle Bone Script character "为", which is the original word of "爲", consists of the component "又" and a pictograph resembling a person using his hand to control the trunk of an elephant, directing it to work for human. This conveys the meaning of making use of an elephant for human. The traditional forms "為" and "爲" have been simplified to "为" in modern standardized Chinese writing. It belongs to the category of pictophonetic compound characters.

为（示意图）

第八单元

丶 丿 为 为
1　2　3　4
楷书书写顺序

本义是指役象以助劳。可引申为做、帮助、表示原因或目的、以为、充当、给、替等义。

The original meaning of the character "为" in Oracle Bone Script is to use an elephant to assist in labor. It can be extended to signify doing, helping, for the purpose of, offering, serving as, among other meanings.

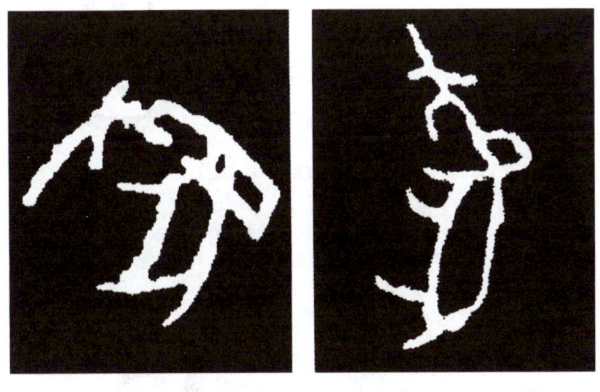

为（甲骨文拓片）

与为组合的词有：为此、为难、为什么、为人师表等。
Compound words related to the character "为" include:
1. 为此（wèi cǐ）– For this; Because of this
2. 为难（wéi nán）– Feel embarrassed or awkward; Be in a difficult situation
3. 为什么（wèi shén me）– Why; For what reason
4. 为人师表（wéi rén shī biǎo）– Serve as a model teacher for others

第九单元

chū

出

甲骨文"出"字，上部为行走之止，代表脚，下方一条曲线表示古人穴居洞穴之门。两形会意表示走出穴居洞门之意。此会走出之意。属会意字。

The Oracle Bone Script character "出" features the upper part representing the walking symbol "止", symbolizing "feet", and the lower part with a curved line indicating the entrance to the cave where ancient people dwelled. The combination of these two elements signifies the act of walking out of the cave entrance, conveying the meaning of departure. This character belongs to the category of ideogram and compound ideogram characters.

出（示意图）

第九单元

丨 凵 屮 出 出
1　2　3　4　5

楷书书写顺序

本义指外出。引申为来到某处、出现、拿出、离开、发出、生出、超过等义。
The original meaning is to go out. It can be extended to arriving at a place, appearing, taking out, leaving, emitting, giving birth, exceeding, and so on.

出（甲骨文拓片）

与出组合的词有：出发、出国、出席、出口成章、出乎意料等。
Compound words related to the character "出" include:
1. 出发（chū fā）– Set out; Depart
2. 出国（chū guó）– Go abroad
3. 出席（chū xí）– Attend
4. 出口成章（chū kǒu chéng zhāng）– Speak eloquently
5. 出乎意料（chū hū yì liào）– Beyond expectation

第九单元

miàn

面

甲骨文"面"字,外部轮廓像是人的一个脸面形,中间是一只大眼睛"目"字。

The Oracle Bone Script character "面" features an outer contour resembling the shape of a human face. In the middle, there is a large eye, forming the character "目"(mù), which represents an eye.

面(示意图)

第九单元

一 𠂇 𠂆 丆 而 而 而 面 面

1 2 3 4 5 6 7 8 9

楷书书写顺序

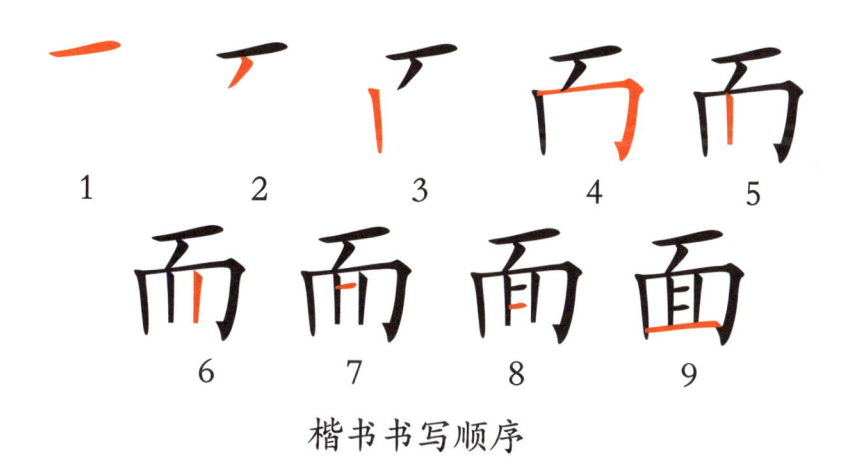

本义指脸面。可引申为事物的外表、面向、侧面、平面、面粉、违背、及事物的量词等义。

The original meaning refers to the face or surface of something. It can be extended to indicate the appearance, orientation, side, plane, flour, violation, and a measure word for certain things.

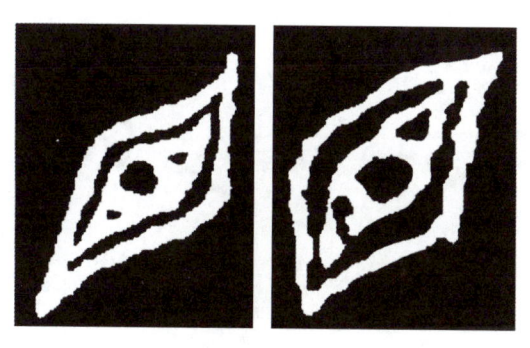

面（甲骨文拓片）

与面组合的词有：面包、面具、面条、面对面、面貌一新等。
Compound words related to the character "面" include:

1. 面包（miàn bāo）– Bread
2. 面具（miàn jù）– Mask
3. 面条（miàn tiáo）– Noodles
4. 面对面（miàn duì miàn）– Face-to-face
5. 面貌一新（miàn mào yī xīn）– A completely new appearance

第九单元

zì
自

甲骨文"自"字,像是人的一鼻子形状。属象形字。一般人们都有以手指自己鼻子代表自己的意思。

The Oracle Bone Script character "自" resembles the shape of a person's nose. Generally, people use the gesture of pointing to their own noses to represent the concept of oneself. It belongs to the category of pictographic characters.

自(示意图)

第九单元

丿 亻 门 自 自 自
1　2　3　4　5　6

楷书书写顺序

本义是指鼻子。可引申为开始、本来、从由、自己、自然等义。

The original meaning refers to the nose. It can be extended to signify the beginning, original state, from, oneself, naturally, and so on.

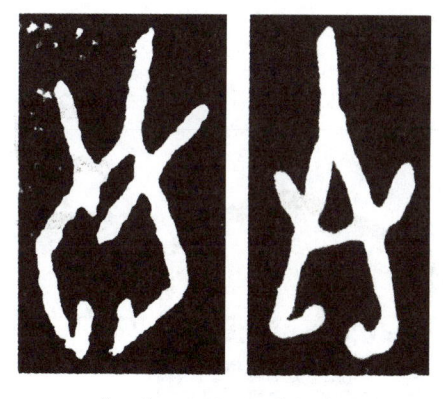

自（甲骨文拓片）

与自组合的词有：自由、自觉、自尊、自然界、自动化、自行车等。

Compound words related to the character "自" include:

1. 自由（zì yóu）– Freedom
2. 自觉（zì jué）– Self-aware
3. 自尊（zì zūn）– Self-respect
4. 自然界（zì rán jiè）– Natural world
5. 自动化（zì dòng huà）– Automation
6. 自行车（zì xíng chē）– Bicycle

第九单元

jǐ
己

甲骨文"己"字，像来回交错把丝绳编系在箭杆之上的丝绳之形。以此表示编结、约束、系联之意。属象形字。

The Oracle Bone Script character "己" depicts the intertwined pattern of silk threads being braided and tied around the shaft of an arrow. This represents the idea of weaving, binding, and connecting. It belongs to the category of pictographic characters.

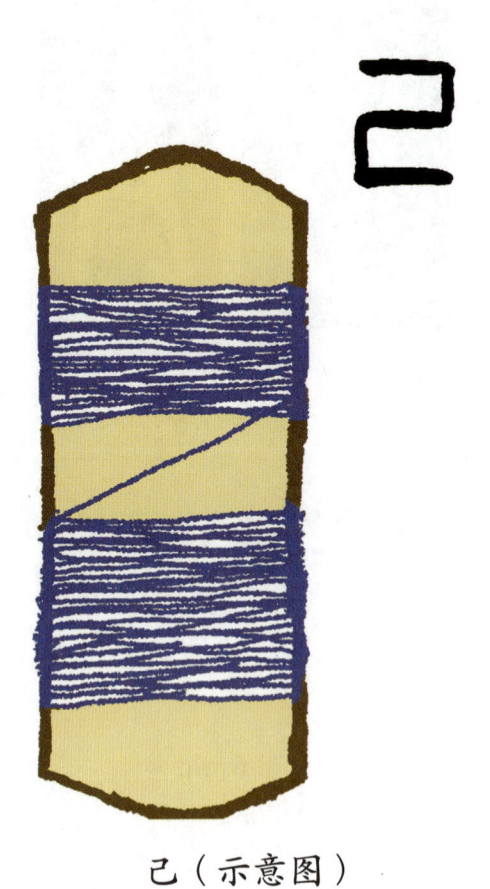

己（示意图）

第九单元

ㄱ ㄋ 己

    1   2   3

楷书书写顺序

    本义是指弯曲的丝绳。可引申为自己、纲领、治理、记载、纪年单位及借用作天干的第六位等义。

The original meaning refers to the silk threads used for making arrow shafts. It can be extended to signify oneself, principles, governance, record-keeping, a unit for recording years, and the sixth position in the Heavenly Stems, among other meanings.

己（甲骨文拓片）

    与己组合的词有：己见、知己知彼、舍己为人、严于律己等。
Compound words related to the character "己" include:
1. 己见（jǐ jiàn）– One's own views
2. 知己知彼（zhī jǐ zhī bǐ）– Know yourself and know your enemy
3. 舍己为人（shě jǐ wèi rén）– Self-sacrifice for others
4. 严于律己（yán yú lù jǐ）– Strict with oneself

第九单元

tóng

同

甲骨文"同"字,从凡,像盘口之形。从口,表示口形。可会两口相合之义,表示齐心合力。属会意字。古造仝字,从人,从工,与同通。

The Oracle Bone Script character "同" consists of the component "凡", resembling the shape of a mouth of a vessel, and the component "口", representing the mouth. The combination of these two elements signifies the idea of two mouths coming together, indicating unity and collaboration. This character belongs to the category of ideogram and compound ideogram characters. In ancient times, the character "仝" was used interchangeably, sharing similarities with "人"(person) and "工"(work), and it was interchangeable with the character "同"。

同(示意图)

第九单元

丨 冂 冂 同 同 同
1　2　3　4　5　6

楷书书写顺序

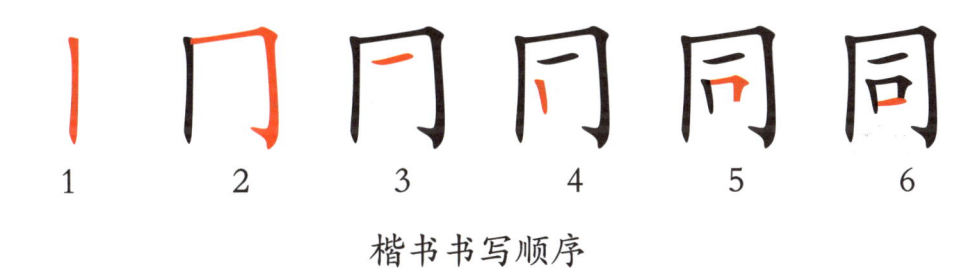

本义是指二口相合。可引申为众人同心合力、会合、共同、相同、一样、和、同情、同志等义。

The original meaning is two mouths coming together. It can be extended to signify people coming together with one heart and one effort, gathering, common, identical, the same, harmony, sympathy, comrades, and so on.

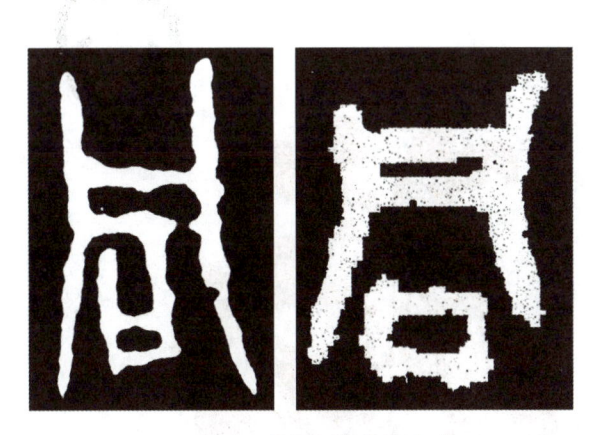

同（甲骨文拓片）

与同组合的词有：同意、同学、同事、同心同德等。
Compound words related to the character"同"include:
1. 同意（tóng yì）– Agree
2. 同学（tóng xué）– Classmate
3. 同事（tóng shì）– Colleague
4. 同心同德（tóng xīn tóng dé）– United and of one mind

第九单元

xīn
心

甲骨文"心"字，像人和动物的心脏之形。上端左右短斜画像心脏上的血管或心脏的瓣膜。属象形字。

The Oracle Bone Script character "心" is a pictographic character, depicting the shape of a human or animal heart. The upper part features short slanting lines on the left and right, resembling blood vessels or the valves of the heart.

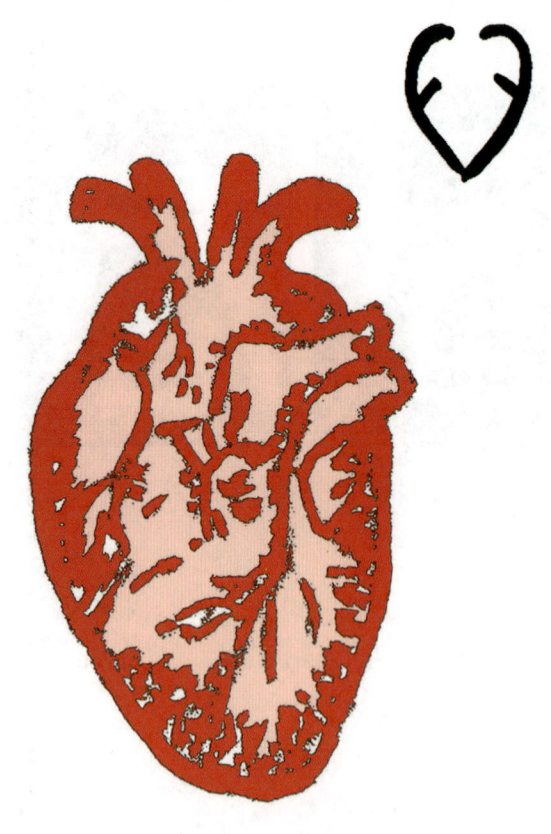

心（示意图）

第九单元

丶 心 心 心
1　2　3　4

楷书书写顺序

本义是指心脏。可引申为思想、胸部、中心、花蕊、心房、心花怒放等义。

The original meaning refers to the heart. It can be extended to signify thoughts, chest, center, flower pistil and stamen, atrium, and expressions like "心花怒放"（heart blooming with joy）。

心（甲骨文拓片）

与心组合的词有：心情、心态、心愿、心跳、心理学、心领神会等。

Compound words related to the character "心" include:

1. 心情（xīn qíng）– Mood
2. 心态（xīn tài）– Mentality
3. 心愿（xīn yuàn）– Wish
4. 心跳（xīn tiào）– Heartbeat
5. 心理学（xīn lǐ xué）– Psychology
6. 心领神会（xīn lǐng shén huì）– Understand without explanation

第九单元

liǎng

两

甲骨文"两"字，合体构型，从鬲，像古代烹煮用的鬲器，腹空，三足分裆，无耳，近似鼎器。可会二鬲并列之形以示"两"之意。"兩"为繁体字，今汉字简化规范写作"两"为正体。属会意字。

The Oracle Bone Script character "两" has a composite structure. It includes the component "鬲", resembling the ancient cooking vessel "鬲器" with an empty belly, three legs spreading apart, and no ears, similar to a tripod cauldron. The character represents the concept of "two" by depicting the form of two "鬲" arranged side by side. This character belongs to the category of ideogram and compound ideogram characters. "兩" and "两" are the traditional scripts, and in modern simplified Chinese, "两" is used as the standard form.

两（示意图）

第九单元

一 丆 门 丙 丙 两 两
1　2　3　4　5　6　7

楷书书写顺序

　　本义为成对的两个。可引申为双、并、对立依存的二面、几、古货币单位等义。

The original meaning refers to a pair of two. It can be extended to signify double, both, the interdependence of opposites, a few, and an ancient unit of currency.

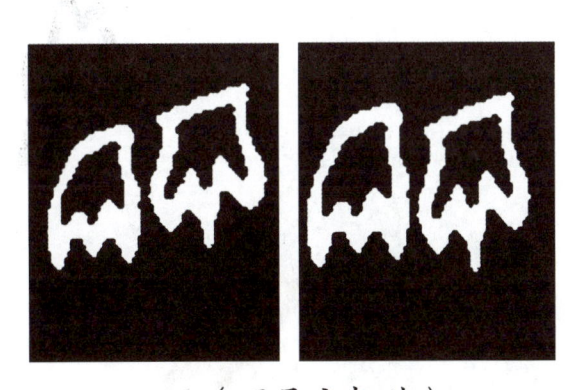

两（甲骨文拓片）

　　与两组合的词有：两手、两国、两侧、两全其美等。
Compound words related to the character "两" include:
1. 两手（liǎng shǒu）– Both hands
2. 两国（liǎng guó）– Two countries
3. 两侧（liǎng cè）– Both sides
4. 两全其美（liǎng quán qí měi）– The best of both worlds

175

第九单元

dé
得

甲骨文"得"字,从又(手)从贝,以手持贝之形,就是获得、得到的意思。又加"行",表示在行路上拾得"贝",属会意字。

The Oracle Bone Script character "得" is formed with the components "又"(hand) and "贝"(shell or valuable item). It depicts the shape of a hand holding a valuable item, representing the meaning of obtaining or gaining. The addition of "行"(to walk) indicates acquiring the "贝" while walking on the road, making it a compound ideogram character.

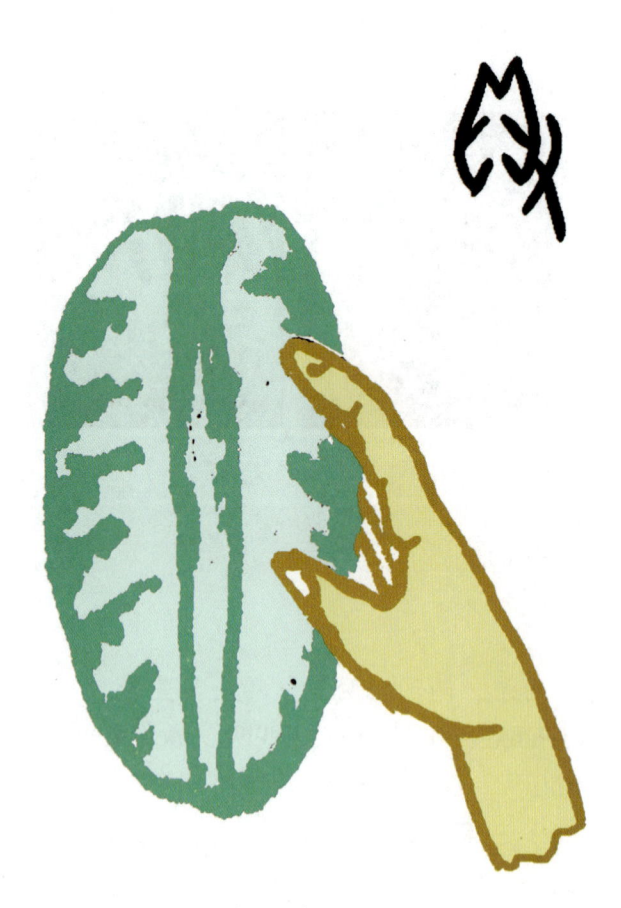

得(示意图)

第九单元

楷书书写顺序

本义是指获得、得到。可引申为得意、中意、取得、应该、可能、正确、具备、必须等义。

The original meaning is to obtain or gain. It can be extended to signify pleased, favored, achieve, should, possible, correct, possess, must, and so on.

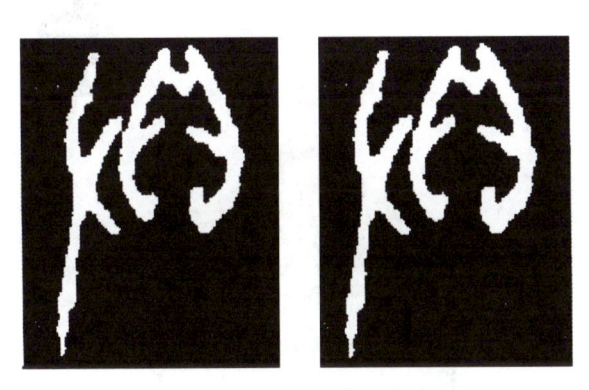

得（甲骨文拓片）

与得组合的词有：得知、得胜、得失、得寸进尺等。
Compound words related to the character "得" include:
1. 得知（dé zhī）– To know; To be informed
2. 得胜（dé shèng）– To win; To be victorious
3. 得失（dé shī）– Gains and losses
4. 得寸进尺（dé cùn jìn chǐ）– Push one's luck

第九单元

jiù

就

甲骨文"就"字,合体构型,上从亯,像古代在高大台基上建造起殿堂、亭台及祭祀宗庙一类建筑物;下从京,像用立柱、土石等为基础建筑物。属会意字。

The Oracle Bone Script character "就" is a compound ideogram. The upper part depicts a structure resembling the construction of palaces, pavilions, and ancestral temples on elevated platforms in ancient times. The lower part resembles the foundation of a building using pillars, earth, and stones.

就(示意图)

第九单元

丶 亠 宀 亣 亣 亨
1　2　3　4　5　6

亨 京 京 訃 就 就
7　8　9　10　11　12

楷书书写顺序

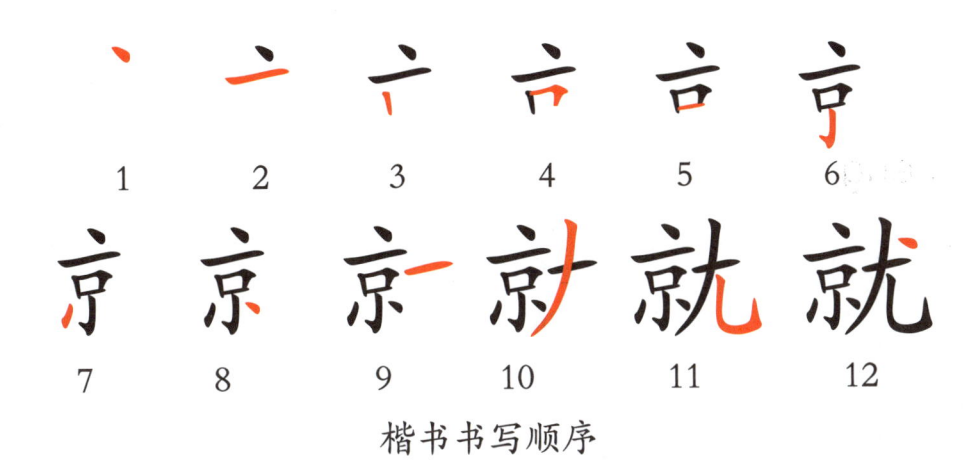

本义是指就高而居、走向高处。可引申为重申、成就、靠近、趋向等义。

The original meaning is to reside at a higher place, ascend to a higher level. It can be extended to signify reiterate, achieve, approach, tend toward, and so on.

就（甲骨文拓片）

与就组合的词有：就业、就位、就绪、就地取材等。
Compound words related to the character "就" include:

1. 就业（jiù yè）– Employment; Take a job
2. 就位（jiù wèi）– Take one's place; Assume a position
3. 就绪（jiù xù）– Be ready; Be prepared
4. 就地取材（jiù dì qǔ cái）– Use local materials; Make use of local resources

néng

能

甲骨文"能"通"熊",像一只长嘴、大耳、巨身、短尾的大狗熊形。后又讹加四点作火旁,成为熊字古文。属象形字。

The Oracle Bone Script character "能" is a pictographic character. It resembles a large bear with a long snout, big ears, a massive body, and a short tail. Later, four dots were added near the fire component, forming the ancient script for the word "熊"（bear）.

能（示意图）

第九单元

厶 厶 亇 台 台 台
1　2　3　4　5　6

台 能 能 能
7　8　9　10

楷书书写顺序

本义为熊类野兽。引申为才能、能力、亲善、够、乃等义。

The original meaning is a bear-like wild animal. It is extended to signify talent, ability, kindness, enough, so, and so on.

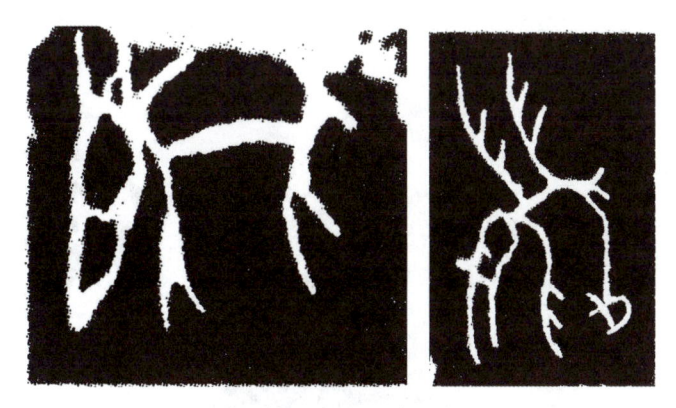

能（甲骨文拓片）

与能组合的词有：能够、能源、能工巧匠、能歌善舞、能说会道等。
Compound words related to the character "能" include:

1. 能够（néng gòu）– To be able to; Capable of
2. 能源（néng yuán）– Energy source
3. 能工巧匠（néng gōng qiǎo jiàng）– Skilled craftsman
4. 能歌善舞（néng gē shàn wǔ）– Proficient in singing and dancing
5. 能说会道（néng shuō huì dào）– Articulate and eloquent

181

第十单元

huán

还

（其他读音：hái）

甲骨文"还"字，从彳或从行，像人行道路口之形。从睘，表示回还之意，兼作表声。隶定为"還"字，可会从路上返回之意。"還"为繁体字，今汉字简化规范写作"还"为正体。属形声会意字。

The Oracle Bone Script character "还" is composed of "彳" (a radical representing walking) or "行" (also a radical related to walking) resembling the intersection of paths or a pedestrian crossing. The component "睘" signifies the idea of returning or repaying, and it also functions as a phonetic indicator. In clerical script, it is evolved into "還", representing the concept of returning from a journey. The traditional character is written as "還", and in modern simplified Chinese, it is written as "还". This character belongs to the category of a compound ideogram and phonogram characters.

还（示意图）

第十单元

一 丁 丆 不 不 还 还
1　2　3　4　5　6　7

楷书书写顺序

本义为返回。可引申为回报、回击、归还、交还、顾虑、反而等义。

The original meaning is to return. It can be extended to signify repayment, counterattack, give back, hand over, concern, on the contrary, and so on.

还（甲骨文拓片）

与还组合的词有：还是、还原、还有、还乡等。
Compound words related to the character "还" include:
1. 还是（hái shì）– Or
2. 还原（huán yuán）– Restore; Reduction
3. 还有（hái yǒu）– Still have; There is also
4. 还乡（huán xiāng）– Return to one's hometown

183

第十单元

立

甲骨文"立"字，像正面站立着一个人，下方一条横线表示大地，象征人站立在地面上之意。属会意字。通"位"。

The Oracle Bone Script character "立", also known as the character "位", depicts a person standing upright facing forward in the upper part, with a horizontal line below representing the earth, symbolizing the idea of a person standing on the ground. It belongs to the category of compound ideogram characters.

立（示意图）

第十单元

丶 亠 亣 亣 立
1　2　3　4　5

楷书书写顺序

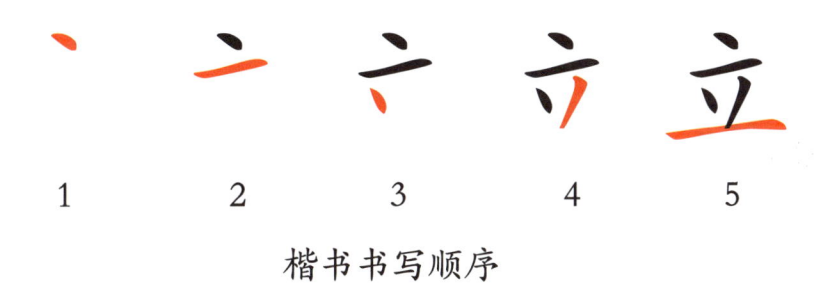

本义指人站立着。可引申为建立、存在、帝王即位义。

The original meaning refers to a person standing upright, and it can be extended to signify establishment, existence, and the enthronement of an emperor.

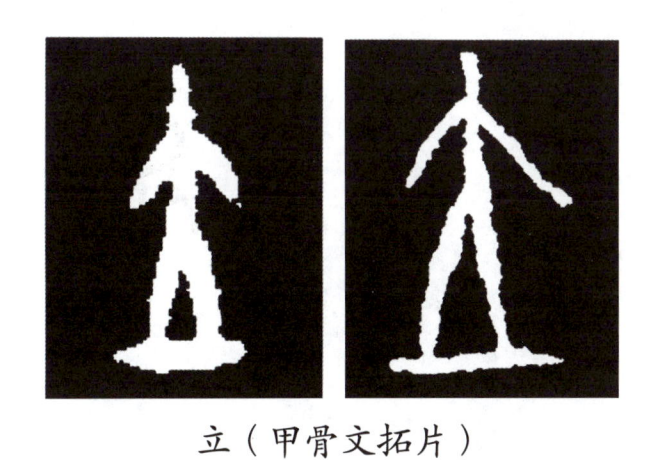

立（甲骨文拓片）

与立组合的词有：立即、立场、立体的、立方米等。
Compound words related to the character "立" include:
1. 立即（lì jí）– Immediately
2. 立场（lì chǎng）– Position; Standpoint
3. 立体的（lì tǐ de）– Three-dimensional
4. 立方米（lì fāng mǐ）– Cubic meter

第十单元

zhǐ
只

甲骨文"只"字,从又,像手之形。从隹,像鸟之形。此可会获抓一鸟之意。为"获"的本字,通假"获"字。属会意字。"隻"为繁体字,今汉字简化规范写作"只"为正体。

The Oracle Bone Script character "只" consists of the component "又", resembling the shape of a hand, and "隹", resembling the shape of a bird. This suggests the meaning of capturing or grasping a bird. It was the original character for "获"（huò）, and was interchangeable with it. This character belongs to the category of compound ideogram characters. "隻" is the traditional form, and in modern simplified Chinese, the standardized character is written as "只".

只（示意图）

第十单元

丶　冂　口　只　只
1　　2　　3　　4　　5

楷书书写顺序

本义是手持一鸟。可引申为"双"相反、仅、孤独、单一的、独特的等义。
The original meaning is to hold a bird with one hand. It can be extended to signify the opposite of paired or double, meaning only, solitary, singular, unique, and so on.

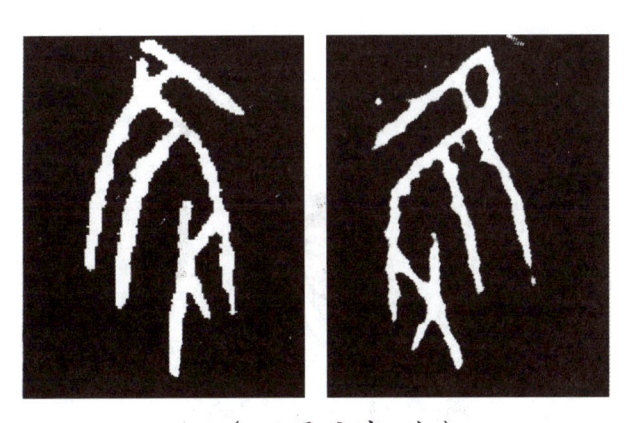

只（甲骨文拓片）

与只组合的词有：只有、只是、只好、只不过、只字不提等。
Compound words related to the character "只" include:

1. 只有（zhǐ yǒu）– Only have; There is only

2. 只是（zhǐ shì）– Only; Merely

3. 只好（zhǐ hǎo）– Have no choice but to; Have to

4. 只不过（zhǐ bù guò）– Only; Merely

5. 只字不提（zhī zì bù tí）– Not mention a word; Keep silent about something

第十单元

xiào

校

甲骨文"校"字，从木，像树木之形。从交，本像两腿交叉正立之人形，这里作标声。两形会意表示用两木相交制作的刑具，即枷。属会意形声字。

The Oracle Bone Script character "校" consists of the component "木", representing the shape of a tree. The component "交" originally depicted the form of a person standing upright with legs crossed, serving as a phonetic component here. It signifies a punitive instrument made by crossing two pieces of wood, namely a cangue. This character belongs to the category of compound ideogram and phonogram characters.

校（示意图）

第十单元

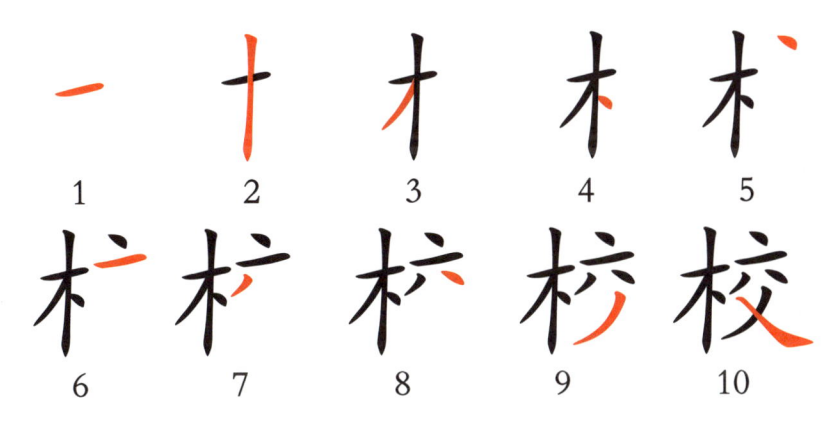

楷书书写顺序

本义为古代刑具枷。引申为学校、栅栏、考核、查对、军衔名、比较、习武场地等义。

The original meaning refers to the ancient punitive instrument, the cangue. It is extended to signify school, fence, assessment, verification, military ranks, comparison, martial arts practice grounds, and so on.

校（甲骨文拓片）

与校组合的词有：校长、校门、校园、校友会等。
Compound words related to the character "校" include:
1. 校长（xiào zhǎng）– Principal（of a school）
2. 校门（xiào mén）– School gate
3. 校园（xiào yuán）– Campus
4. 校友会（xiào yǒu huì）– Alumni association

第十单元

xǐ
喜

甲骨文"喜"字，从壴（表示鼓），从口，会为击鼓呈欢笑之意。属会意字。

The Oracle Bone Script character "喜" consists of the component "壴" representing a drum and the component "口" representing a mouth. Together, they symbolize the action of drumming to express joy and laughter. This character belongs to the category of compound ideogram characters.

喜（示意图）

第十单元

楷书书写顺序

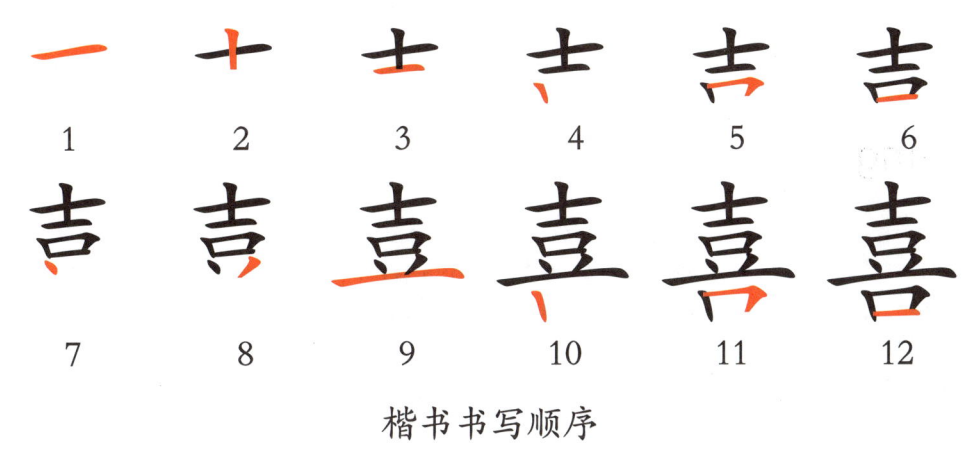

本义应指欢乐、喜悦。可引申为爱好、适宜于、可喜可贺等义。

The original meaning refers to joy and happiness. It can be extended to signify fondness, suitability, and something worthy of congratulations, and so on.

喜（甲骨文拓片）

与喜组合的词有：喜欢、喜剧、喜鹊、喜洋洋等。
Compound words related to the character "喜" include:
1. 喜欢（xǐ huān）– Like; Be fond of
2. 喜剧（xǐ jù）– Comedy
3. 喜鹊（xǐ què）– Magpie
4. 喜洋洋（xǐ yáng yáng）– Full of joy and happiness

第十单元

jīng
京

甲骨文"京"字,像用立柱、土石等为基础建筑物,在其上再筑亭屋、塔台,又似高筑瞭望哨所,以观敌情、以察民事。属象形字。

The Oracle Bone Script character "京" resembles the construction of buildings with pillars, soil, and stones as the foundation, upon which pavilions, towers, and platforms are built. It also resembles the construction of watchtowers for observing enemy movements and civil affairs. This character belongs to the category of pictographic characters.

京(示意图)

第十单元

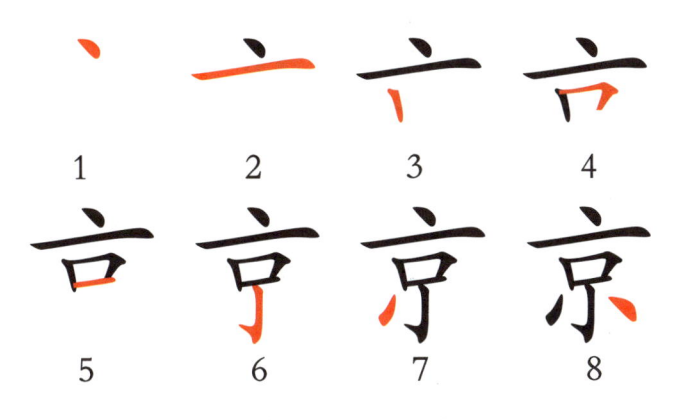

亠 亠 亠 亠
1　2　3　4

亠 亣 亣 京
5　6　7　8

楷书书写顺序

本义是指楼阁亭屋。可引申为大谷仓、高大的、京城、首都等义。

The original meaning refers to buildings such as towers and pavilions. It can be extended to signify granaries, tall and large structures, as well as capital cities and capitals.

京（甲骨文拓片）

与京组合的词有：北京、南京、京城、京杭大运河等。
Compound words related to the character"京"include:

1. 北京（běi jīng）– Beijing
2. 南京（nán jīng）– Nanjing
3. 京城（jīng chéng）– Capital city; Capital
4. 京杭大运河（jīng-háng dà yùn hé）– Grand Canal（Beijing-Hangzhou Grand Canal）

193

第十单元

xí

习

甲骨文"刁"即"習"字，从羽，羽即"彗"字，本像扫帚形，这里表示鸟双羽在空中飞翔之意。从日，像太阳之形，这里表示晴日、白天。此可会飞鸟在天气晴好的空中展翅反复练习之意。属会意字。"習"为繁体字，今汉字规范简化写作"习"为正体。

The Oracle Bone Script character "刁", also written as "習", consists of the component "羽", which represents wings or feathers, originally depicted as a broom shape, indicating the flight of birds with their wings in the air. The component "日" resembles the shape of the sun, representing clear weather or daytime. The combination symbolizes the idea of birds repeatedly practicing flying in fine weather. This character belongs to the category of compound ideogram characters. The traditional character is written as "習", and in modern simplified Chinese, it is written as "习".

习（示意图）

第十单元

㇆ ㇆ 习
1　2　3
楷书书写顺序

本义是指飞鸟展翅反复练习。可引申为学习、熟悉、习惯、经常、重复等义。

The original meaning refers to birds spreading their wings and repeatedly practicing flying. It can be extended to signify learning, familiarity, habit, regularity, repetition, and so on.

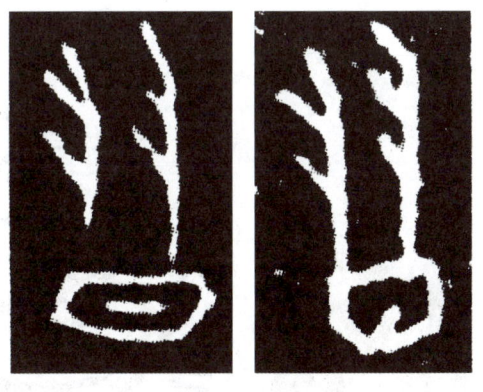

习（甲骨文拓片）

与习组合的词有：习惯、习俗、习题、习气、实习生、习以为常等。
Compound words related to the character"习"include:

1. 习惯（xí guàn）– Habit
2. 习俗（xí sú）– Custom
3. 习题（xí tí）– Exercise（in a textbook）
4. 习气（xí qì）– Bad habit
5. 实习生（shí xí shēng）– Intern
6. 习以为常（xí yǐ wéi cháng）– To become accustomed to something

195

第十单元

tīng

听

甲骨文"听"字,从耳,从口或从双口无别,表示有声之言咏,以耳感知声音则为听。此可会以口说耳闻之意。属会意字。"聽"为繁体字,今汉字简化规范写作"听"为正体。

The Oracle Bone Script character "听" consists of the component "耳" representing the ear and the component "口" or doulbe "口" indicating the sound of speech. This composition signifies the perception of sound by the ear, which is then interpreted as listening. This character belongs to the category of compound ideogram characters. The traditional character is written as "聽", and in modern Chinese, it is written as "听".

听(示意图)

第十单元

丨 冂 口 口⁻ 叿 听 听

1　2　3　4　5　6　7

楷书书写顺序

本义指用耳朵接受声音。可引申为听从、允许、等候、任凭、治理、喜悦、记数、间谍等义。

The original meaning refers to the act of receiving sound with the ears. It can be extended to signify obedience, permission, waiting, allowance, governance, joy, counting, espionage, and so on.

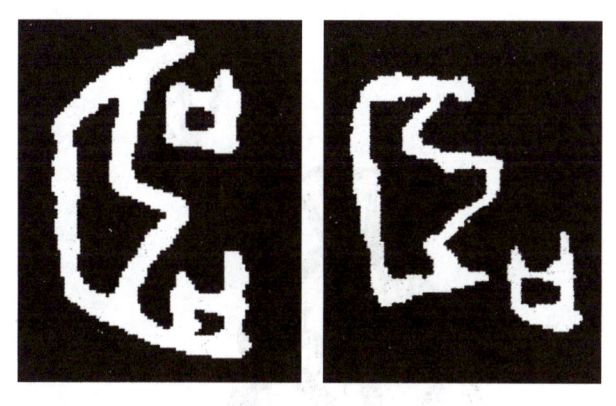

听（甲骨文拓片）

与听组合的词有：听说、听话、听课、听写、听诊器等。

Compound words related to the character "听" include:

1. 听说（tīng shuō）– Heard
2. 听话（tīng huà）– Obedient
3. 听课（tīng kè）– Attend a class
4. 听写（tīng xiě）– Dictation
5. 听诊器（tīng zhěn qì）– Stethoscope

197

第十单元

dōng

东

甲骨文"东"字,像两头扎起来装满货物的大口袋。假借为方位字东,表示东方之义。属象形字。"東"为繁体字,今汉字简化规范写作"东"为正体。

The Oracle Bone Script character "东" depicts a large sack filled with goods and tied up at both ends. It also represents the direction of the east, conveying the concept of the east. This character belongs to the category of pictogram characters. The traditional character is written as "東", and in modern Chinese, it is written as "东".

东(示意图)

第十单元

一 𠂆 𣎳 东 东
1　2　3　4　5

楷书书写顺序

本义为口袋。可引申为主人、太阳升起处、东道主等义。

The original meaning is a sack or pouch and can be extended to signify the host, the place where the sun rises, or the host of an event.

东（甲骨文拓片）

与东组合的词有：东方、东欧、东南亚、东山再起、东张西望等。
Compound words related to the character "东" include:
1. 东方（dōng fāng）– The East; The Orient
2. 东欧（dōng ōu）– Eastern Europe
3. 东南亚（dōng nán yà）– Southeast Asia
4. 东山再起（dōng shān zài qǐ）– Make a comeback
5. 东张西望（dōng zhāng xī wàng）– Look around in all directions

199

第十单元

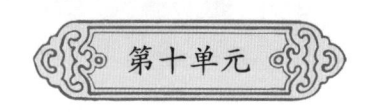

xī

西

甲骨文"西"字，像鸟巢形，日在西方鸟要进巢，鸟在巢里栖息。借巢形表示西方并通"栖"字。卜文巢上有不封口也有封口巢。属象形字。

The Oracle Bone Script character "西" resembles the shape of a bird's nest, indicating the direction of the west. This character is a pictogram, representing the concept of a bird's nest and extended to signify the west. In addition, there are Oracle Bone Inscriptions of "西" with both open and closed nests.

西（示意图）

第十单元

一 厂 兀 丙 西 西
1　2　3　4　5　6

楷书书写顺序

本义是指鸟巢。可引申为日落处、西欧式的、西方、居住、栖息、忙碌等义。

The original meaning refers to a bird's nest and can be extended to signify the place where the sun sets, Western-style, the west, residence, habitat, or busyness.

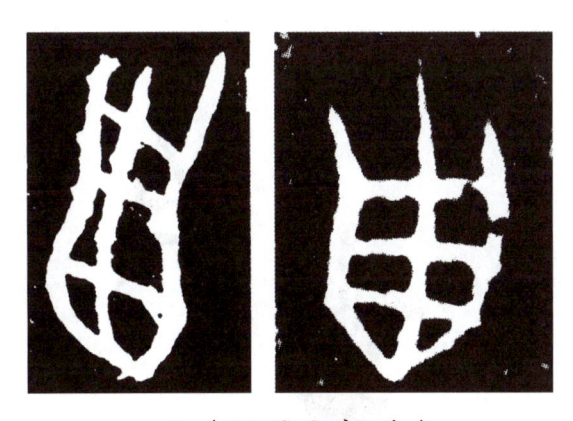

西（甲骨文拓片）

与西组合的词有：西部、西门、西瓜皮、西游记、西班牙等。

Compound words related to the character "西" include:

1. 西部（xī bù）– West
2. 西门（xī mén）– West Gate
3. 西瓜皮（xī guā pí）– Watermelon rind
4. 西游记（xī yóu jì）– *Journey to the West*（a classic Chinese novel）
5. 西班牙（xī bān yá）– Spain

第十一单元

nán
南

甲骨文"南"字,像是悬挂式钟镈一类的空心打击乐器,上为悬状结节绳纽,下为钟体。属象形字。

The Oracle Bone Script character "南" resembles a suspended bell-shaped percussion instrument, with a nodular rope at the top and a bell-shaped body below. This character is a pictogram, representing the concept of a bell, and extended to signify the south.

南(示意图)

第十一单元

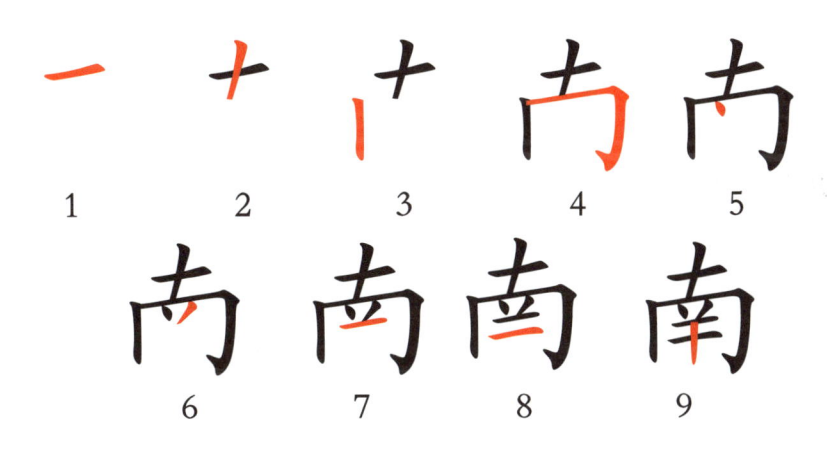

一 十 十 冎 冎
1　2　3　4　5

冎 南 南 南
6　7　8　9

楷书书写顺序

本义应指钟镈。可引申为方位字、南方的乐舞等义。

The original meaning refers to a bell-shaped percussion instrument. It can be extended to denote the direction south and also to represent the music and dance from the southern regions.

南（甲骨文拓片）

与南组合的词有：南极、南海、南美洲、南半球等。

Compound words related to the character "南" include:

1. 南极（nán jí） – The South Pole
2. 南海（nán hǎi） – South China Sea
3. 南美洲（nán měi zhōu） – South America
4. 南半球（nán bàn qiú） – Southern Hemisphere

第十一单元

běi
北

甲骨文"北"字,像二人相背之形,会背离之意。属会意字。

The Oracle Bone Script character "北" depicts the shape of two people facing away from each other, indicating the concept of departing or facing opposite directions. This character is a compound ideogram, representing the idea of moving away or departing.

北(示意图)

第十一单元

丨	十	才	北	北
1	2	3	4	5

楷书书写顺序

本义指两人相背。引申为脊背、北方、败走等义。中原地区的房屋建筑都背北向南,遂引申为北方之北。

The original meaning refers to two people facing away from each other, and it can be extended to denote the back, the north direction, or retreating. In the Central Plains region, houses are traditionally built with their backs to the north and facing south, which further extends the meaning to represent the direction of north.

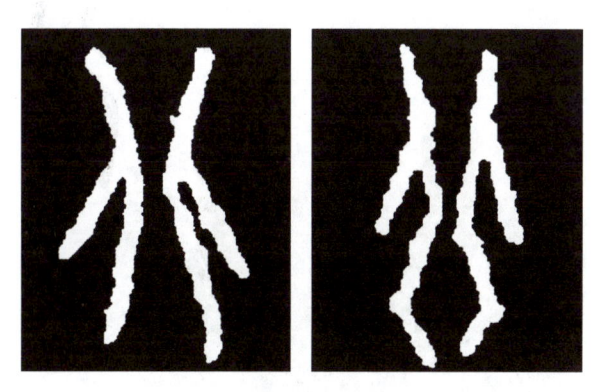

北(甲骨文拓片)

与北组合的词有:北京、北方、北极、北欧、北纬、北斗星等。
Compound words related to the character "北" include:
1. 北京(běi jīng)- Beijing
2. 北方(běi fāng)- North, Northern region
3. 北极(běi jí)- North Pole
4. 北欧(běi ōu)- Northern Europe
5. 北纬(běi wěi)- North latitude
6. 北斗星(běi dǒu xīng)- Big Dipper; Ursa Major

第十一单元

bǐ
比

甲骨文"比"字，从二匕，为二跪拜之人，像比肩之象，表示二人步调一致，比肩而行。会比肩亲近之意。属会意字。

The Oracle Bone Script character "比" depicts two kneeling figures, resembling the concept of standing shoulder to shoulder, indicating that two people are walking together in unison. This character is a compound ideogram, symbolizing the idea of walking side by side in harmony or being close companions.

比（示意图）

第十一单元

一 上 上 比
1　2　3　4

楷书书写顺序

本义是指相比、亲密。可引申为并列、相连接、近来、较量、比方、两相对照等义。

The original meaning refers to comparison or intimacy. It can be extended to denote juxtaposition, connection, recent events, competition, analogy, or comparison between two things.

比（甲骨文拓片）

与比组合的词有：比例、比赛、比武、比喻、比翼双飞等。

Compound words related to the character "比" include:

1. 比例（bǐ lì）– Proportion; Ratio
2. 比赛（bǐ sài）– Competition; Match
3. 比武（bǐ wǔ）– Martial arts competition
4. 比喻（bǐ yù）– Metaphor
5. 比翼双飞（bǐ yì shuāng fēi）– Fly wing to wing, metaphorically referring to a couple flying together in harmony

第十一单元

rú

如

甲骨文"如"字,从口,代表嘴之形状,从女,像一跪跽之女人的形状,并两手交叉置于腹前。会听命、顺从的女人之意。口字部与女字部左右位置调换,其义不变。属会意字。

The Oracle Bone Script character "如" consists of two parts: "口" representing the shape of a mouth, and "女" depicting the figure of a kneeling woman with crossed hands placed in front of her abdomen. This composition symbolizes a woman who listens obediently and complies with orders. By interchanging the positions of the "口" and "女" components, the meaning remains unchanged. This character belongs to the category of compound ideogram characters.

如(示意图)

第十一单元

く　夂　女　如　如　如
1　　2　　3　　4　　5　　6

楷书书写顺序

本义是指遵从、听命。可引申为往、去、如同、比、及、如果、然等义。
The original meaning refers to compliance or obedience. It can be extended to denote going, departing, similarity, likeness, comparison, and, if, in case, and so on.

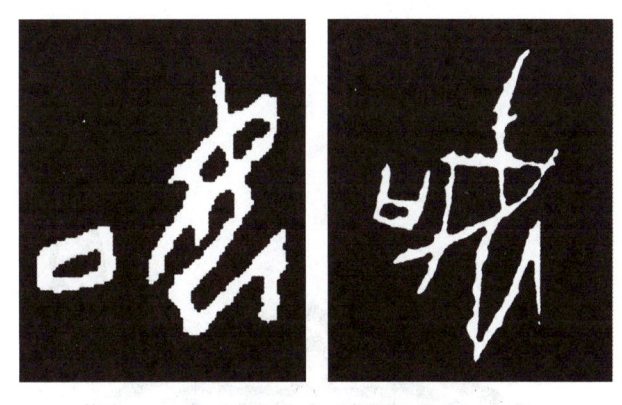

如（甲骨文拓片）

与如组合的词有：如果、如意、如此、如今、如何是好、如梦初醒等。
Compound words related to the character "如" include:

1. 如果（rú guǒ）– If
2. 如意（rú yì）– As desired
3. 如此（rú cǐ）– Like this; Thus
4. 如今（rú jīn）– Nowadays; Now
5. 如何是好（rú hé shì hǎo）– What to do
6. 如梦初醒（rú mèng chū xǐng）– Like waking from a dream; Come to one's senses

第十一单元

zuì

最

甲骨文"最"是"撮"的本字,从月,像房屋之形。从取,像用手抓住耳朵之形。两形会意表示在屋子里用手抓耳朵之意。属象形会意字。"冣"是异体字,今汉字汉字简化规范写作"最"为正体。

The Oracle Bone Script character "最", which is the original word for "撮", comprises two components: "月", resembling the shape of a house, and "取", resembling the action of grabbing the ear with a hand. The combination of these two components conveys the idea of grabbing the ear inside a house. It belongs to the category of ideogrammic compound characters. "冣" is the variant character, and it is simplified as "最" in modern standard writing.

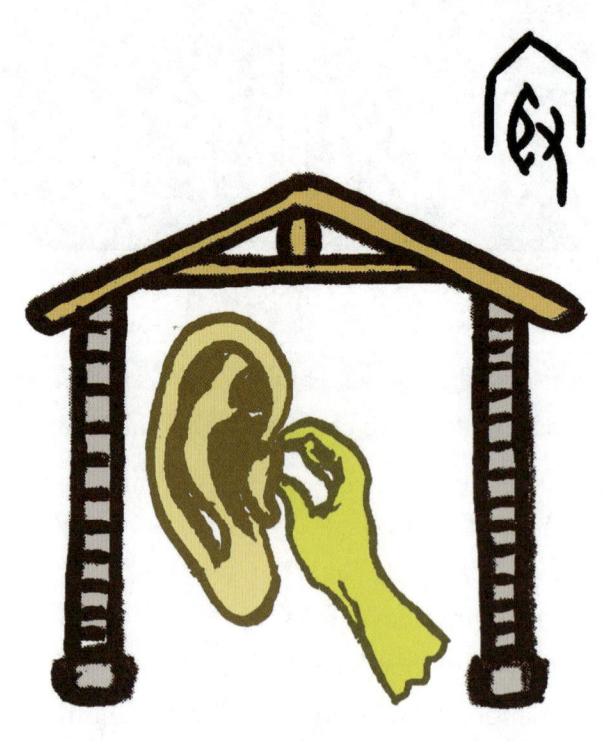

最(示意图)

第十一单元

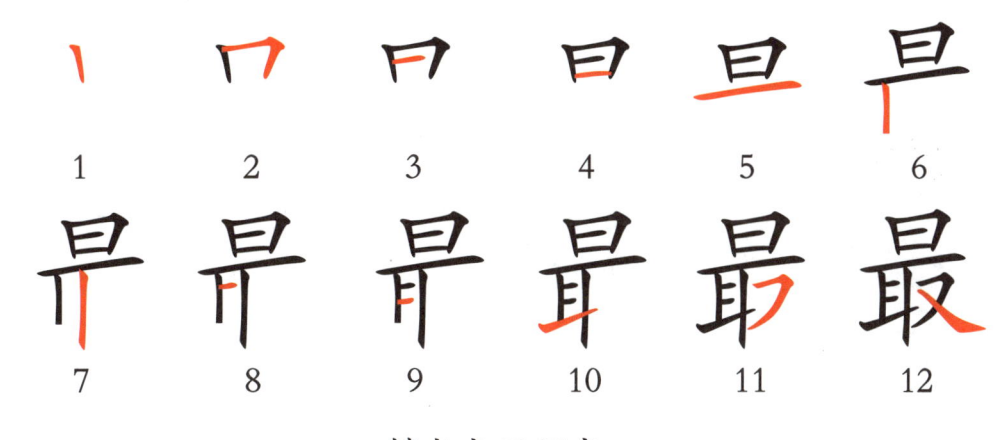

楷书书写顺序

本义是指用手抓住耳朵。引申为极、无比的、聚集、上、大等义。

The original meaning refers to grabbing the ear with a hand. It is extended to mean extreme, incomparable, gathering, top, large, and other meanings.

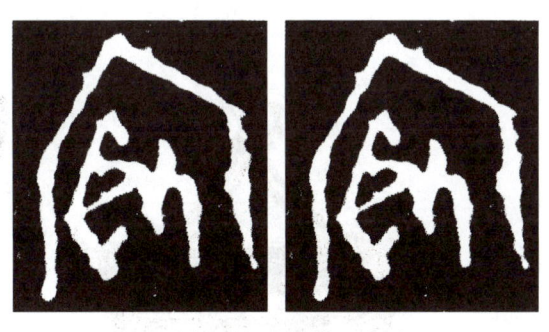

最（甲骨文拓片）

与最组合的词有：最后、最大、最高、最近、最新、最高峰等。

Compound words related to the character "最" include:

1. 最后（zuì hòu）– Last; Final
2. 最大（zuì dà）– Biggest; Largest
3. 最高（zuì gāo）– Highest; Tallest
4. 最近（zuì jìn）– Closest; Nearest
5. 最新（zuì xīn）– Newest; Latest
6. 最高峰（zuì gāo fēng）– Summit; Peak

211

gāo

高

甲骨文"高"字,像观台之楼阁,其上下屋楼高台重叠,以表崇高状。属象形字。

The character "高" in Oracle Bone Script resembles a lookout tower or pavilion with upper and lower floors stacked on top of each other, representing a lofty and elevated structure. It belongs to ideogram characters.

高(示意图)

第十一单元

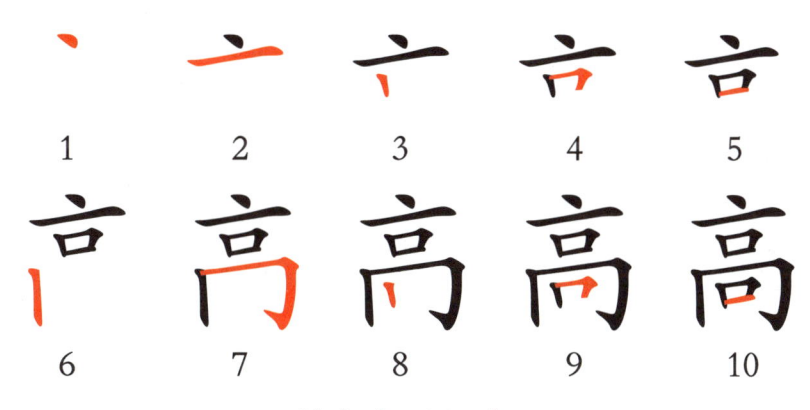

楷书书写顺序

本义为高台。可引申为超出一般水平的、敬辞、大、深远、高低、高大、高远、声音响、岁数大等义。

The original meaning is a high platform. It can be extended to refer to things that exceed the usual level, as a respectful form of address, something large or profound, height, grandeur, loudness of sound, or advanced age.

高（甲骨文拓片）

与高组合的词有：高速、高原、高峰、高雅、高山流水等。

Compound words related to the character "高" include:

1. 高速（gāo sù）– High-speed
2. 高原（gāo yuán）– Plateau
3. 高峰（gāo fēng）– Peak
4. 高雅（gāo yǎ）– Elegant
5. 高山流水（gāo shān liú shuǐ）– Lofty mountains and flowing water（figuratively, referring to high-level artistic achievement）

第十一单元

míng
名

甲骨文"名"字，上下结体（有左右结体），下端从口（有口在左或右），表示在呼唤。上端从月（有月在左或右）。两形会意，表示在夜晚时人们相遇，无法看清对方是谁，需呼叫名字才相认之意。这就是"名"的由来。属会意字。

The character "名" in Oracle Bone Script consists of two parts: the upper part depicts "月" (moon), which may appear on the left or right, and the lower part depicts "口" (mouth), which may also appear on the left or right. Together, they convey the idea of calling out to someone. This combination suggests a situation where people encounter each other at night and cannot see each other clearly, so they need to call out names to recognize each other. This is the origin of the character "名". It belongs to the category of ideographic compound characters.

名（示意图）

第十一单元

丿 夕 夕 夕 名 名
1　2　3　4　5　6

楷书书写顺序

本义是指呼叫名字。可引申为出名、讲出、具有、名称、名望等义。
The original meaning refers to calling out a name. It can be extended to mean fame, mention, possession, title, reputation, and so on.

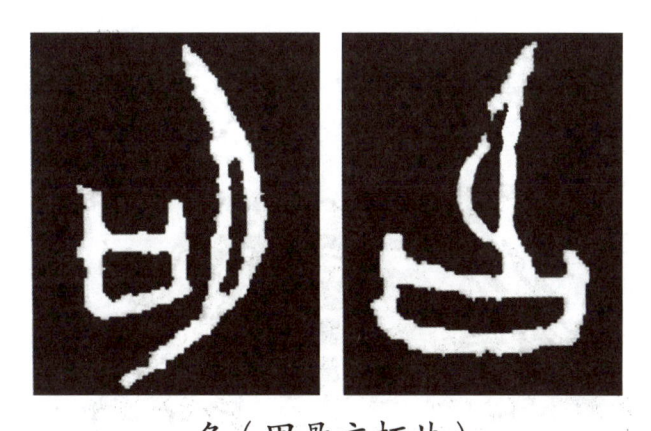

名（甲骨文拓片）

与名组合的词有：名望、名著、名片、名山大川等。
Compound words related to the character "名" include:
1. 名望（míng wàng）– Reputation; Fame
2. 名著（míng zhù）– Famous work; Masterpiece
3. 名片（míng piàn）– Name card; Business card
4. 名山大川（míng shān dà chuān）– Famous mountains and rivers

第十一单元

fù

复

　　甲骨文"复"字，上方像穴居两侧有台阶出入之形，亦像古代城邑之形，下边从倒止，为一脚趾形，像脚围绕城邑往来之意。属会意字。"復"为繁体字，今汉字简化规范写作"复"为正体。

　　The character "复" in Oracle Bone Script depicts a structure resembling a dwelling with steps on both sides, similar to the shape of ancient cities. Below it is a reversed "止", representing a toe-like shape, indicating the movement of feet around the city. This character is a compound ideogram. The simplified form of "復" is written as "复" in modern Chinese script.

复（示意图）

216

第十一单元

丿 𠂉 𠂉 𠂉 𠂉
1　2　3　4　5

𠂉 复 复 复
6　7　8　9

楷书书写顺序

本义指来去往返。可引申为回答、实践、免除、再、夹衣等义。

The original meaning refers to coming and going, back and forth. It can be extended to mean reply, practice, exempt, again, lined garment, etc.

复（甲骨文拓片）

与复组合的词有：复杂、复兴、复印、复制品等。
Compound words related to the character "复" include:
1. 复杂（fù zá）– Complex
2. 复兴（fù xīng）– Revive; Rejuvenate
3. 复印（fù yìn）– Photocopy
4. 复制品（fù zhì pǐn）– Replica; Copy

dàn

旦

甲骨文"旦"字，上下构型，从日从口，日代表太阳，口代表日影。以日与其影若接若离之形表示日刚升起地面之形。会早晨日出时天亮之意。属会意字。

The Oracle Bone Script character "旦" consists of two parts: "日"（sun）on the top and "口"（mouth）below. The "日" represents the sun, and the "口" represents its shadow. The combination of the sun and its shadow suggests the image of the sun rising just above the horizon, indicating the break of dawn. This character signifies the moment when the sun rises and the day begins. It belongs to the category of ideographic characters.

旦（示意图）

第十一单元

丨 冂 冃 日 旦
1　2　3　4　5

楷书书写顺序

本义是指早晨日出。可引申为早晨、明亮、初一、天、日、戏曲角色、诚实等义。

The original meaning refers to the sunrise in the morning. It can be extended to signify morning, brightness, the first day of the month, sky, the sun, roles in traditional Chinese opera, honesty, and so on.

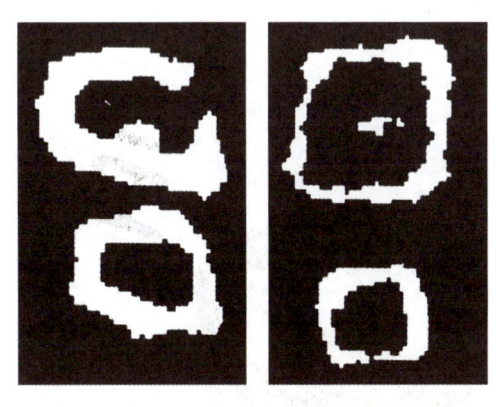

旦（甲骨文拓片）

与旦组合的词有：元旦、旦夕、圣诞、震旦、复旦大学等。

Compound words related to the character"旦"include:

1. 元旦（yuán dàn）– New Year's Day
2. 旦夕（dàn xī）– Day and night; Dawn and dusk
3. 圣诞（shèng dàn）– Holy dawn; Christmas Day
4. 震旦（zhèn dàn）– An ancient name for China
5. 复旦大学（fù dàn dà xué）– Fudan University（a university in Shanghai）

第十一单元

duō

多

　　甲骨文"多"字，像叠置的两块肉，我国古代祭祀为赐胙肉，以分二块，二块为数量之多。属会意字。

　　The character "多" in Oracle Bone Script resembles two pieces of stacked meat. In ancient China, during sacrificial ceremonies, the sacrificial meat was divided into two pieces, representing a large quantity. This character is a compound ideogram.

多（示意图）

第十一单元

丿 ク 夕 夕 多 多
1　2　3　4　5　6

楷书书写顺序

本义是指肉多。引申为推崇、赞美、过多、剩余、数量大、相差程度大等义。

The original meaning refers to a large amount of meat. It can be extended to mean admiration, praise, excessive, surplus, large quantity, and significant difference in degree.

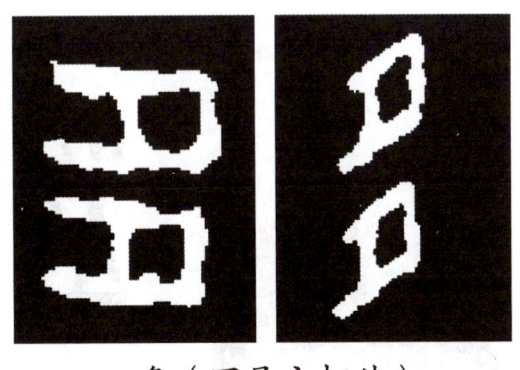

多（甲骨文拓片）

与多组合的词有：多数、多彩、多云、多谢、多样性、多姿多彩等。
Compound words related to the character "多" include:

1. 多数（duō shù）– Majority
2. 多彩（duō cǎi）– Colorful; Diverse
3. 多云（duō yún）– Cloudy
4. 多谢（duō xiè）– Many thanks
5. 多样性（duō yàng xìng）– Diversity
6. 多姿多彩（duō zī duō cǎi）– Varied and colorful

duì
对

甲骨文"对"字,像点燃的三组蜡烛火具,人面对并用手执持辉煌之火具。此会高举张扬之意。火是人类生存发展之源,人离不开它。属会意字,"對"为繁体字,今汉字简化规范写作"对"为正体字。

The character "对" in Oracle Bone Script resembles three groups of lit candles, with a person facing them and holding a radiant object with a hand. This symbolizes a gesture of lifting and displaying. Fire is essential for human survival and development, and humans cannot do without it. This character belongs to the category of ideographic characters. "對" is the traditional form, and its simplified form in modern Chinese writing is "对".

对(示意图)

第十二单元

マ 又 又 对 对
1　2　3　4　5

楷书书写顺序

本义是对火、高举显扬。引申为相当、正确、互相、配偶、平分、敌对朝着、不错、比照、对付等义。

The original meaning is holding up and displaying fire. It is extended to signify equivalence, correctness, mutual, spouse, equal sharing, facing opposition, right, comparison, dealing with, and other meanings.

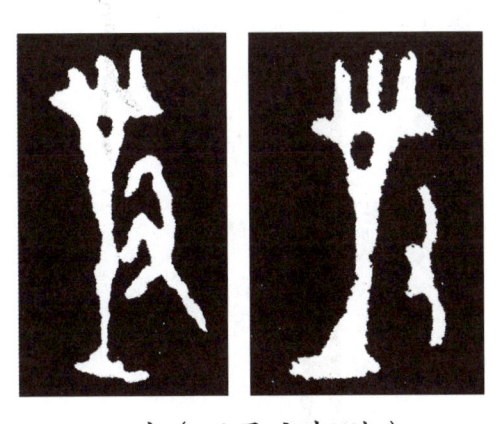

对（甲骨文拓片）

与对组合的词有：对面、对象、对抗、对照等。
Compound words related to the character "对" include:
1. 对面（duì miàn）– Opposite side
2. 对象（duì xiàng）– Object; Target
3. 对抗（duì kàng）– Confrontation; Resistance
4. 对照（duì zhào）– Comparison; Contrast

第十二单元

fāng

方

甲骨文"方"字，像是起土出粪的大锸形，其上方代表扶把，中间横画代表足踏着力部分，下方代表锸口铲头，属象形字。

The Oracle Bone Script character "方", resembles the shape of a large spade used for digging up soil and removing manure. The upper part symbolizes the handle for support, the horizontal stroke in the middle represents the part where one steps on to exert force, and the lower part stands for the shovel head of the spade. It is a pictographic character.

方（示意图）

第十二单元

丶 亠 方 方
1　2　3　4

楷书书写顺序

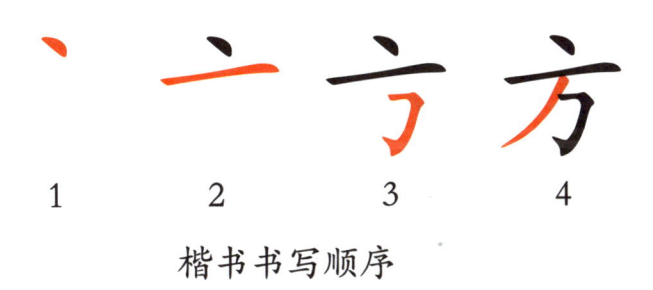

本义是指起土之铲锸。可引申为方形、正直、大地、地方、方向、药方、途径、方圆面积、义理、正在等义。

The original meaning refers to a shovel for digging up soil. It can be extended to mean square, upright, land, place, direction, prescription, way, area, principle, currently, and so on.

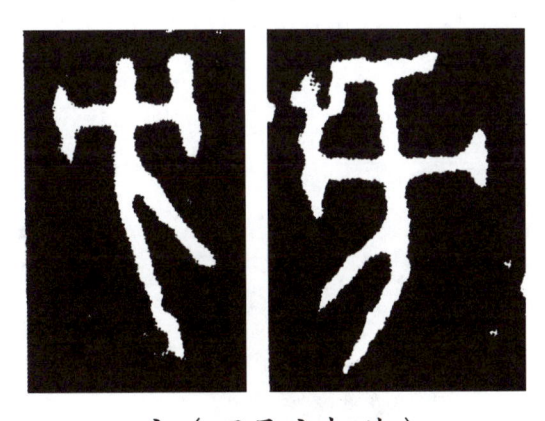

方（甲骨文拓片）

与方组合的词有：方向、方法、方便、方向盘、方便面等。

Compound words related to the character "方" include:

1. 方向（fāng xiàng）– Direction
2. 方法（fāng fǎ）– Method
3. 方便（fāng biàn）– Convenient
4. 方向盘（fāng xiàng pán）– Steering wheel
5. 方便面（fāng biàn miàn）– Instant noodles

第十二单元

zuǒ
左

甲骨文"左"字,像左手形,上部代表手指形,下部代表手臂形。从金文开始下方加了"工"字,表示辅助右手干活之意,故左通佐字。属象形字。

The character "左" in Oracle Bone Script is a pictographic character. It resembles the shape of a left hand, with the upper part representing the fingers and the lower part representing the arm. In later bronze inscriptions, the character was modified with the addition of the character "工" below, indicating the auxiliary function of the left hand while the right hand is engaged in work, hence "左" is related to the concept of assisting or being subordinate, and was interchangeable with the character "佐".

左(示意图)

第十二单元

一　ナ　ナ　ナ　左
1　2　3　4　5

楷书书写顺序

本义为左手。引申为与"右"相对之左方、帮助、辅助、不正、偏斜、证据、不正派、不协调、降职等义。古人面南站立时，左手在东边，故古人以东为左。

The original meaning of "左" refers to the left hand, and it is extended to mean the left side in contrast to the right, assistance, support, deviation, evidence, misconduct, inconsistency, demotion, and so on. In ancient times, when people stood facing south, the left hand was toward the east, hence in ancient culture, the east was considered the left side.

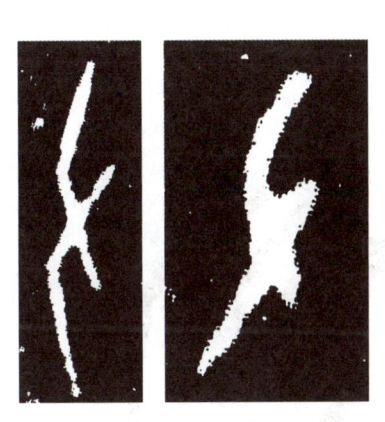

左（甲骨文拓片）

与左组合的词有：左耳、左下角、左右为难等。
Compound words related to the character "左" include:
1. 左耳（zuǒ ěr）– Left ear
2. 左下角（zuǒ xià jiǎo）– Lower left corner
3. 左右为难（zuǒ yòu wéi nán）– Caught in a dilemma

第十二单元

yòu

右

甲骨文"右"字，像右手之形。上部像手指头，下部像手臂形。属象形会意字。通"又"字。

The character "右" in Oracle Bone Script is an ideogrammic compound character. It resembles the shape of a right hand, with the upper part representing the fingers and the lower part representing the arm. It was interchangeable with the character "又".

右（示意图）

第十二单元

一 ナ ナ 右 右
1　2　3　4　5

楷书书写顺序

本义指右手。引申为与左相对之右方、重复、连续、并列、递进、再加上、补充、轻微转折、强调等义。

The original meaning of "右" refers to the right hand, and it is extended to mean the right side in contrast to the left, repetition, continuation, parallelism, progression, addition, supplementation, slight turn, emphasis, and so on.

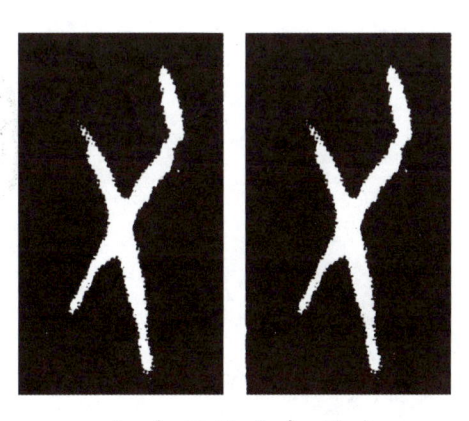

右（甲骨文拓片）

与右组合的词有：右手、右边、右下角、座右铭、左右逢源等。
Compound words related to the character "右" include:
1. 右手（yòu shǒu）- Right hand
2. 右边（yòu bian）- Right side
3. 右下角（yòu xià jiao）- Lower right corner
4. 座右铭（zuò yòu míng）- Motto; Maxim
5. 左右逢源（zuǒ yòu féng yuán）- Favorable on both sides

tā

它

甲骨文"蛇"字即"它"字,互相通假。其形像是一条蛇状。属象形字。

The Oracle Bone Script character "蛇" is also the character "它". They are interchangeable. This character belongs to the category of pictograms. Its shape resembles that of a snake.

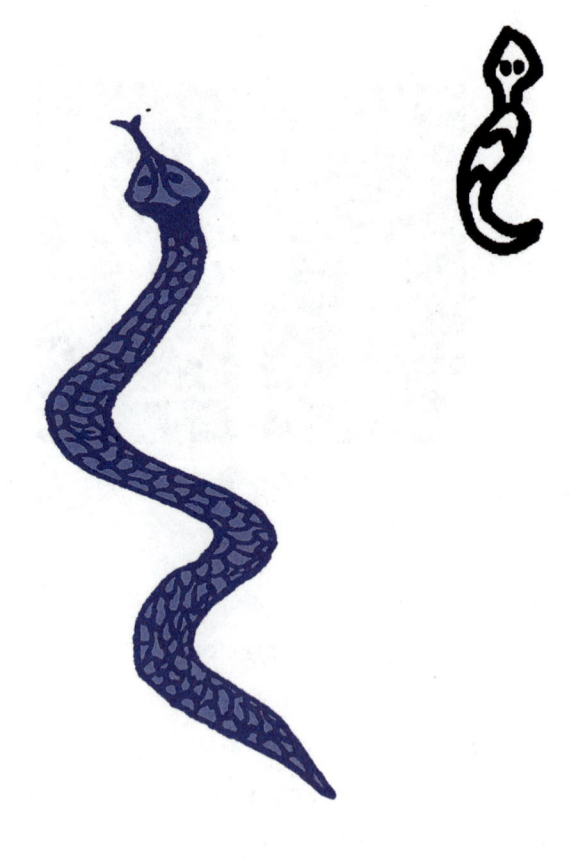

它(示意图)

第十二单元

丶 丷 宀 宀 它
1　2　3　4　5

楷书书写顺序

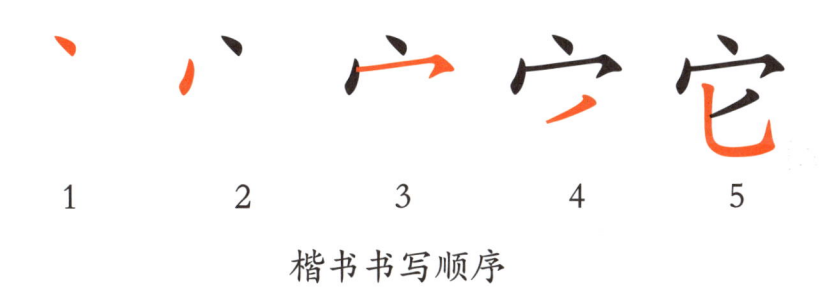

本义是指蛇。可引申为别的、人或物、负荷、第三人称、不确定的指代等义。

The original meaning of the Oracle Bone Script character "它" refers to a snake. It can be extended to mean other, person or thing, load, third person, indefinite reference, and so on.

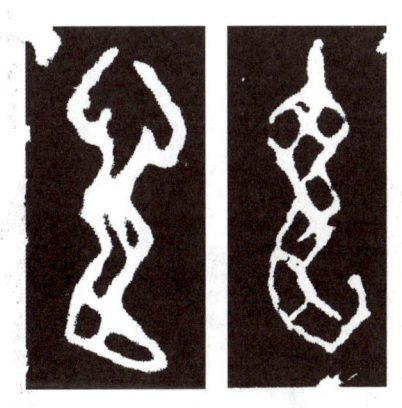

它（甲骨文拓片）

与它组合的词有：它日、其它、它山之石等。
Compound words related to the character "它" include:
1. 它日（tā rì）– Another day
2. 其它（qí tā）– Other; Another
3. 它山之石（tā shān zhī shí）– A stone from another mountain (meaning advice from others)

第十二单元

zhī
知

甲骨文"知"字,从示,像神台牌位之形。从矢,像箭形。从口,像在神台神主前陈述战争与和平之政事。属会意字。通假"智"字。

The Oracle Bone Script character "知" consists of three parts: "示"(shì), which represents an altar or shrine, "矢"(shǐ), which resembles an arrow, and "口"(kǒu), which depicts the act of speaking. Together, they signify presenting political matters related to war and peace before the gods or spirits at the shrine. This character is a compound ideogram and is interchangeable with "智"(zhì), meaning intelligence or wisdom.

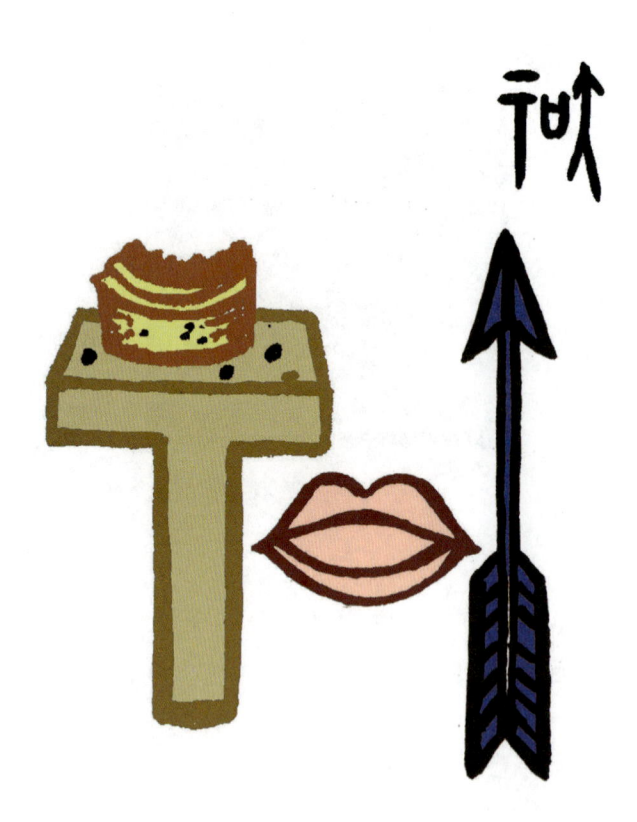

知(示意图)

232

第十二单元

丿 亻 与 午 矢 知 知 知
1　2　3　4　5　6　7　8

楷书书写顺序

本义指讨论政事，陈述知识。引申为智慧、才识、知觉、学问、主管、使其知道等义。

The original meaning of the Oracle Bone Script character "知" refers to discussing political affairs and presenting knowledge. It can be extended to mean wisdom, knowledge, perception, scholarship, authority, and making someone aware of something.

知（甲骨文拓片）

与知组合的词有：知己、知音、知足、知书达理等。
Compound words related to the character "知" include:
1. 知己（zhī jǐ）– Intimate friend
2. 知音（zhī yīn）– Kindred spirit; Soulmate
3. 知足（zhī zú）– Content; Satisfied
4. 知书达理（zhī shū dá lǐ）– Knowledgeable and reasonable

dào

道

甲骨文"道"字，从行，像人行道路口之形。从人，像人之侧视形。表示人行走在大路上之意。属会意字。

The character "道" in Oracle Bone Script consists of two components: "行" and "人". "行" represents the concept of walking or a pathway, resembling the intersection of pathways. "人" depicts a side view of a person. Together, they signify a person walking along a main road or pathway. This character is a compound ideogram.

道（示意图）

第十二单元

丶 丷 䒑 䒑 产 产
1　2　3　4　5　6

首 首 首 首 道 道
7　8　9　10　11　12

楷书书写顺序

本义指行道。可引申为路程、行程、规律、方向、途径、道德、方法、主张、述说等义。

The original meaning of the character "道" in Oracle Bone Script refers to a pathway. It can be extended to mean journey, course, rule, direction, approach, morality, method, principle, discourse, and so on.

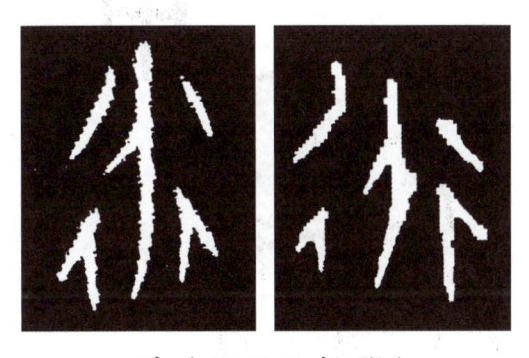

道（甲骨文拓片）

与道组合的词有：道教、道义、道具、道德观等。

Compound words related to the character "道" include:

1. 道教（dào jiào）- Taoism
2. 道义（dào yì）- Morality; Righteousness
3. 道具（dào jù）- Props; Equipment
4. 道德观（dào dé guān）- Moral perspective

第十二单元

yòng

用

甲骨文"用"字，中间有卜字部，故应为从卜。以表示骨版上有卜兆，可依其用之行事。属会意字。

The Oracle Bone Script character "用" features the component "卜" in the middle, indicating its derivation from "卜". This suggests that on oracle bones, there were divinations（"卜兆"）that could guide actions, hence representing the concept of usage or application. It belongs to the category of compounds ideogram characters.

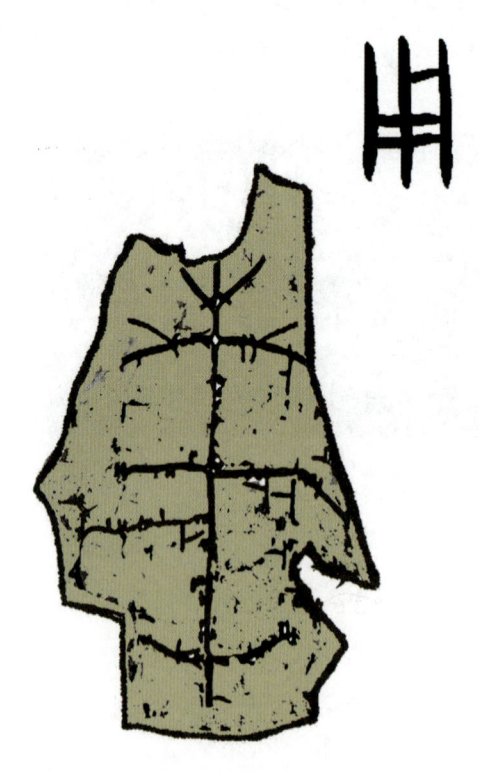

用（示意图）

第十二单元

丿 冂 冃 月 用
1　2　3　4　5

楷书书写顺序

本义是指依据卜兆行事。可引申为任用、吃喝、作用、需要、凭借等义。

The original meaning refers to acting according to divinations. It can be extended to mean using, employing, consuming, functioning, needing, relying on, and so on.

用（甲骨文拓片）

与用组合的词有：用户、用途、用心、用法等。
Compound words related to the character"用"include:
1. 用户（yòng hù）– User
2. 用途（yòng tú）– Use; Application
3. 用心（yòng xīn）– Careful; Attentive
4. 用法（yòng fǎ）– Usage

第十二单元

lín

林

甲骨文"林"字，从二木，双木为林，古代以二为多数。此可会树木有很多之意。属会意字。

The character "林" in Oracle Bone Script consists of two "木"（mù）, meaning trees. The repetition of "木" implies a multitude of trees, symbolizing a forest. It is a compound ideogram conveying the concept of a dense collection of trees.

林（示意图）

238

第十二单元

一 十 才 木 木 朴 材 林
1 2 3 4 5 6 7 8

楷书书写顺序

本义是指树林。可引申为林业、森林、树林、竹林、盛貌、隐居地、聚集在一起的事物等义。

The original meaning refers to a forest or woods. It can be extended to mean forestry, forest, woods, bamboo grove, flourishing, a place of seclusion, or a gathering of things together.

林（甲骨文拓片）

与林组合的词有：林立、林场、林林总总等。
Compound words related to the character "林" include:
1. 林立（lín lì）– Stand in great numbers
2. 林场（lín chǎng）– Forest farm
3. 林林总总（lín lín zǒng zǒng）– Various and numerous

239

第十二单元

sēn
森

甲骨文"森"字，从三木，排列形式稍有不同，有三木鼎立排列、有三木并列式排列。此可会树木汇聚在一起之意，表示树木众多，成为森林之意。属会意字。

The character "森" in Oracle Bone Script is formed by three "木", arranged slightly differently, either in a triangular or parallel layout. It signifies the gathering of trees or the abundance of trees, indicating a forest. "森" belongs to compound ideogram characters.

森（示意图）

第十二单元

1	2	3	4	5	6
一	十	才	木	木	木

7	8	9	10	11	12
朩	朩	森	森	森	森

楷书书写顺序

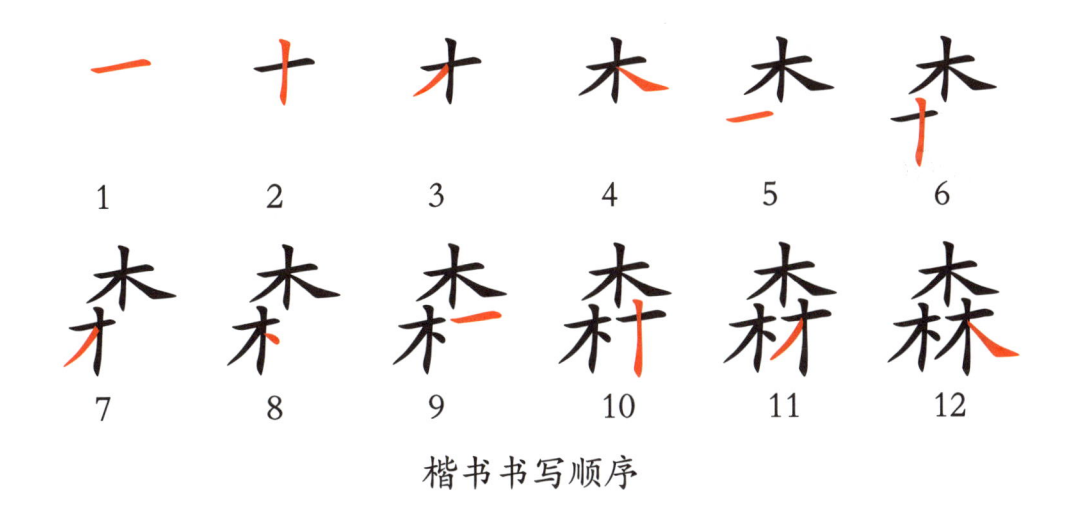

本义指有众多的树木重叠地生长在一起。可引申为众多、严整、森严、阴沉、幽暗、繁密、整齐等义。

The original meaning likely refers to numerous trees growing densely together. It can be extended to signify abundance, strictness, solemnity, darkness, denseness, and neatness, among other meanings.

森（甲骨文拓片）

与森组合的词有：森林、戒备森严等。
Compound words related to the character "森" include:
1. 森林（sēn lín）– Forest; Woods
2. 戒备森严（jiè bèi sēn yán）– Heavily guarded

shēn

身

甲骨文"身"字，好似一大肚子怀着孕的人形。属象形字。从人而隆其腹，或以示其有了身孕，孕妇之腹特大，故身亦可指腹，腹为人体主要部分。

The character "身" in Oracle Bone Script resembles the shape of a person with a large pregnant belly. It is a pictographic character. The depiction emphasizes the swollen belly, indicating pregnancy. Since the abdomen is a main part of the human body, "身" can also refer to the abdomen.

身（示意图）

第十三单元

丶 亻 丬 勹 自 身 身
1　2　3　4　5　6　7

楷书书写顺序

本义应指身孕。可引申为躯体、主体、本身、亲自、自身的品德和生命、物体的主体等义。

The original meaning of the character "身" refers to pregnancy. It can be extended to mean body, main body, oneself, one's own moral character and life, the main body of an object, and so on.

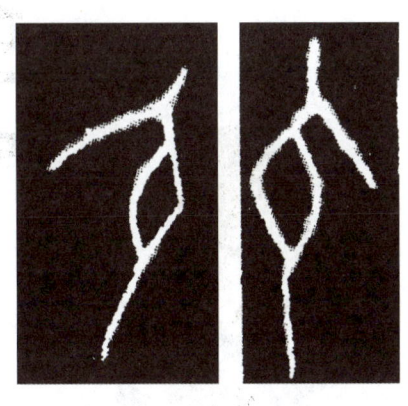

身（甲骨文拓片）

与身组合的词有：身旁、身份、身份证、身心健康等。
Compound words related to the character "身" include:
1. 身旁（shēn páng）– Beside
2. 身份（shēn fèn）– Status; Identity
3. 身份证（shēn fèn zhèng）– Identity Card
4. 身心健康（shēn xīn jiàn kāng）– Physical and mental health

第十三单元

qǐ

起
（通"跽"）

甲骨文"起"字，上从己，借作声符。下从止，代表足。指表示挺着上身两腿跪着之意。属象形会意字。通假"跽"字，兼表起始之意。

In Oracle Bone Script, the upper part of the character "起"."己", serves as a phonetic component, while the lower part, "止", represents the feet. This character depicts a person holding his upper body with his legs bent. It is a pictophonetic compound character. "起" can also be interchangeable with "跽", conveying the idea of beginning or starting.

起（示意图）

第十三单元

一 十 土 キ キ
1　2　3　4　5

走 走 起 起 起
6　7　8　9　10

楷书书写顺序

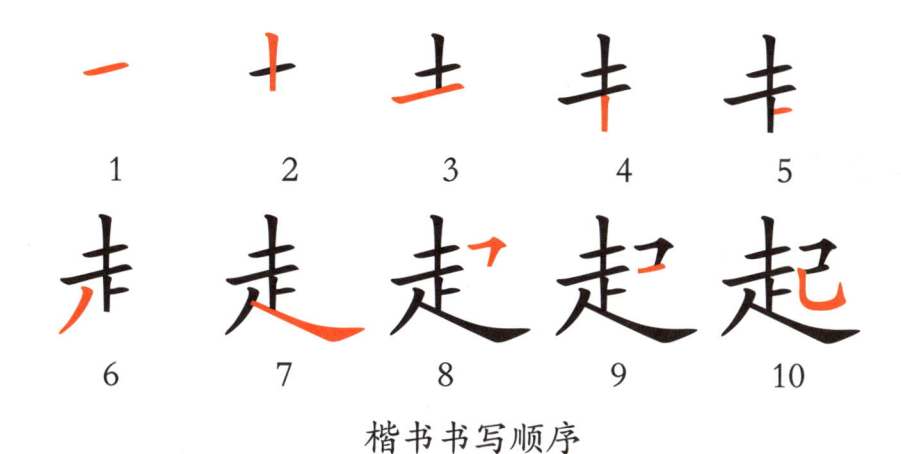

本义指跪踞之意。引申为站立、离开、移动、上升、开始、发生、建立等义。

The original meaning refers to the act of kneeling. It can be extended to mean standing up, leaving, moving, rising, beginning, happening, establishing, and so forth.

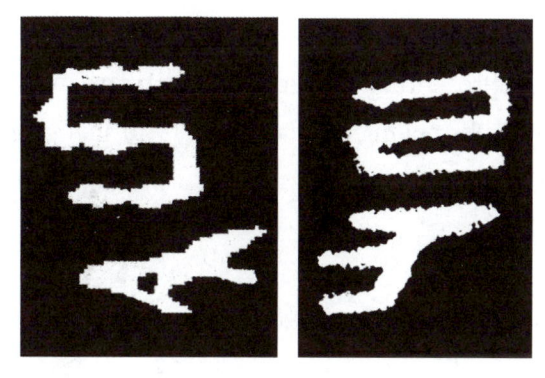

起（甲骨文拓片）

与起组合的词有：起立、起床、起飞、起源、发起等。

Compound words related to the character "起" include:

1. 起立（qǐ lì）– Stand up
2. 起床（qǐ chuáng）– Get up
3. 起飞（qǐ fēi）– Take off
4. 起源（qǐ yuán）– Origin
5. 发起（fā qǐ）– Initiate

第十三单元

chéng
成

甲骨文"成"字，从戈，表示长柄斧钺之器。下方从｜，表示像一块木状之物。两形会意，即以斧劈物，表示成盟。有从丁者（一方口形）除兼表声外，亦表示兵丁将领举斧在手，斩物以誓盟之意。如折箭为誓、歃血定盟类，皆为古人订约斩物成盟之习俗，或称古代建交仪式。属会意字。

The character "成" in Oracle Bone Script is composed of two parts: "戈", representing a long-handled axe or weapon, and "｜", representing things in the shape of wood. This combination symbolizes the act of using an axe to split an object, representing the concept of "forming an alliance" or "establishing a covenant." Additionally, when the character includes "丁" (depicting the shape of a mouth), it not only serves as a phonetic component but also suggests soldiers or leaders holding axes in their hands, ready to solemnize an alliance by chopping objects. This practice, akin to making vows with broken arrows or smearing the blood as a sign of oath, reflects the ancient custom of formalizing alliances through ritualistic acts such as chopping objects, representing an ancient form of treaty-making or diplomatic ceremonies. This character belongs to the category of ideographic compounds.

成（示意图）

第十三单元

一 厂 厂 成 成 成
1　2　3　4　5　6

楷书书写顺序

本义是指媾和、和解。可引申为完成、变成、促成、成型的、可以、达到、有能力、现成的、十分之一等义。

The original meaning of the character "成" is to unite or reconcile. It can be extended to signify completion, transformation, accomplishment, formation, capability, availability, attainment, readiness, one-tenth, and so forth.

成（甲骨文拓片）

与成组合的词有：成语、成功、成群结队等。

Compound words related to the character "成" include:

1. 成语（chéng yǔ）– Chinese idiom
2. 成功（chéng gōng）– Success
3. 成群结队（chéng qún jié duì）– In groups and in large numbers

247

第十三单元

cì
次

甲骨文"次"字，从人，像人跪跽之形，张着口，作吹奏之状。口前二点为指事符，表示第二。可会吹奏水准非第一，仅二等或次等之意。属指事字。

The character "次" in Oracle Bone Script consists of the "人"（person）radical, depicting a person kneeling and blowing, with two dots in front of the mouth, which means the second. This implies that the person is playing a musical instrument, and her skill could rank only second or inferior. It belongs to the category of indicative characters.

次（示意图）

第十三单元

丶 冫 冫 冫 冫 次
1　2　3　4　5　6

楷书书写顺序

本义指居次、第二的。引申为次第、依次、第二、质量较差、停留、中间、接连、至、及等义。

The original meaning refers to being in the second position or rank. It is extended to imply sequence, order, second, inferior quality, stay, interval, consecutive, to, and so on.

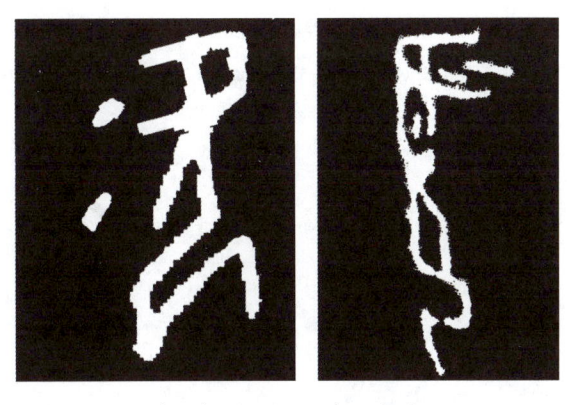

次（甲骨文拓片）

与次组合的词有：次要、次日、次序、三番两次等。
Compound words related to the character "次" include:
1. 次要（cì yào）– Secondary
2. 次日（cì rì）– The next day
3. 次序（cì xù）– Order; Sequence
4. 三番两次（sān fān liǎng cì）– Repeatedly

第十三单元

jìn

进

甲骨文"进"字，从隹，像鸟之形。从止，像脚趾之形。表示鸟脚在地上行走时只能前进不能后退之意，而且鸟能飞善行，故可会前进之意。属会意字。"進"为繁体字，今汉字简化规范写作"进"为正体。

The Oracle Bone Script character "进" consists of two parts: "隹", resembling the shape of a bird, and "止", resembling the shape of toes. It shows that birds' feet can only move forward but not backward when they are walking on the ground. Additionally, birds are known for their ability to fly and move skillfully, hence "进" also means advancing or moving forward. It belongs to the category of compound ideographic characters. The traditional form "进" is "進", which is simplified according to modern Chinese character simplification standards, now written as "进" in standard script.

进（示意图）

第十三单元

一 二 ㄏ 丗 丗 讲 进
1　2　3　4　5　6　7

楷书书写顺序

本义指前进。引申为献出、提出、出仕、举荐、超越、晋升、收入、呈上等义。

The original meaning of the character "进" refers to advancing or moving forward. It is extended to imply actions such as offering, presenting, serving, recommending, surpassing, promoting, receiving, and submitting.

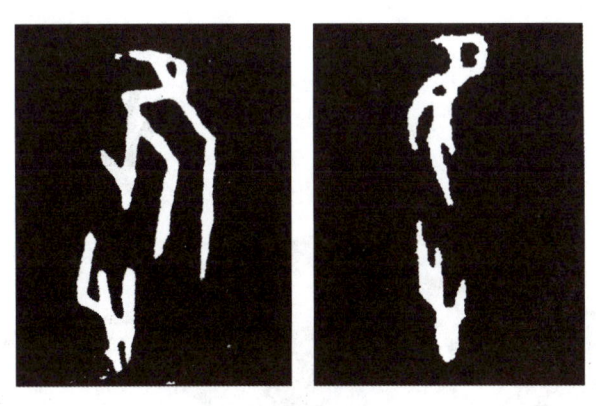

进（甲骨文拓片）

与进组合的词有：进步、进攻、进取、进球、进进出出等。
Compound words related to the character "进" include:
1. 进步（jìn bù）– Progress; Advance
2. 进攻（jìn gōng）– Attack; Assault
3. 进取（jìn qǔ）– Enterprising; Enterprising spirit
4. 进球（jìn qiú）– Score a goal
5. 进进出出（jìn jìn chū chū）– In and out

第十三单元

zuò

作

甲骨文"作"字,是"乍"的初文。像制作衣服之初,仅成领襟之形,带"丰"之形符者,以代表手持针缝纫之线迹,突出并夸张线迹置未成之衣上,会制作之意。属会意字。

The character "作" in Oracle Bone Script originates from the character "乍". It resembles the initial stage of making clothes, only forming the shape of a collar. When adding "丰", it represents the visible and exaggerated stitching lines on the unfinished clothes, indicating the act of making. It belongs to the category of ideographic characters.

作(示意图)

第十三单元

丿 亻 亻 作 作 作 作
1　2　3　4　5　6　7

楷书书写顺序

本义是指缝作领襟。可引申为制作、起始、竖起、惊动、初始、突然、担任、场所、调料等义。

The original meaning refers to sewing collars. It can be extended to mean making, starting, erecting, startling, initiating, suddenly, assuming, place, seasoning, etc.

作（甲骨文拓片）

与作组合的词有：作用、作者、作客、作业本等。
Compound words related to the character "作" include:
1. 作用（zuò yòng）– Function; Effect
2. 作者（zuò zhě）– Author; Writer
3. 作客（zuò kè）– Be a guest
4. 作业本（zuò yè běn）– Exercise book; Workbook

dì

第

甲骨文"第"即"弟"字,从弋,像是一系丝绳缠绕于弋杆上之形,此可会次第缠绕之意。初之"第"字从竹、弟声,或省声,为"弟"字的本字。通弟。属假借会意字。

The character "第" in Oracle Bone Script is equivalent to "弟" and originates from "弋", resembling a series of threads winding around a stalk. This suggests the concept of winding in sequence. Originally, "第" was written with the bamboo radical and the sound component of "弟", or without the sound component, as the original character "弟". Hence, "第" is interchangeable with "弟", functioning as a borrowed ideogram.

第(示意图)

第十三单元

丿 ⺅ ⺊ ⺮ ⺮ ⺮
1　2　3　4　5　6

笁 笁 笁 笁 第
7　8　9　10　11

楷书书写顺序

本义为缠绕的次第。可引申为辈分低的男性、弟子、次第、等级、科第、朋友等义。

The original meaning is the sequence of winding. It can be extended to refer to younger male siblings, disciples, sequence, hierarchy, grades, friends, etc.

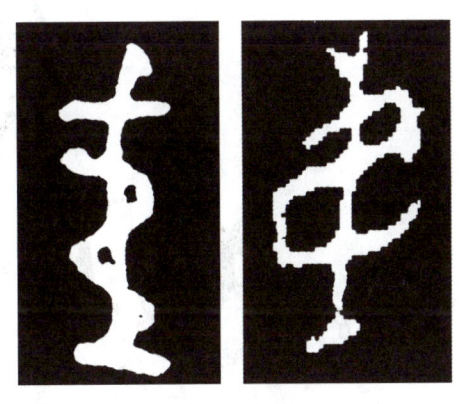

第（甲骨文拓片）

与第组合的词有：第一、第二、书香门第等。
Compound words related to the character "第" include:
1. 第一（dì yī）– First
2. 第二（dì èr）– Second
3. 书香门第（shū xiāng mén dì）– A Family of scholars

255

第十三单元

fā

发

（通"發"）

甲骨文"发"即"發"字，从二止，表示两脚趾形。从又，表示手之形。手中之丨为物省，或像手持棍棒之谓。整个字形结体表示两脚脚踏实地，并将两腿叉开，以手持棍棒向前掷去，代表发出的意思。属会意字。"發"为"發"之初文，"發"为繁体字，今简化规范写作"发"为正体。

The Oracle Bone Script character "发" or "發" is a compound ideogram. The component "从" represents two toes, while "又" represents a hand. The vertical line "丨" in the hand symbolizes a weapon or a stick. The entire character depicts two feet firmly on the ground, legs spread apart, with a hand throwing a stick forward, representing the act of "發" or emitting something. "發" is the original form of "發", and in modern Chinese writing, "发" is the standardized form.

发（示意图）

第十三单元

丶 ⺈ 为 发 发
1　2　3　4　5

楷书书写顺序

本义为发出、发射。引申为踏草、送出、发落、表达、发挥、打开、散发、迂回屈曲等义。

The original meaning is to emit or launch. It extends to stepping on grass, sending out, expressing, exerting, opening, emitting, twisting and turning, and so on.

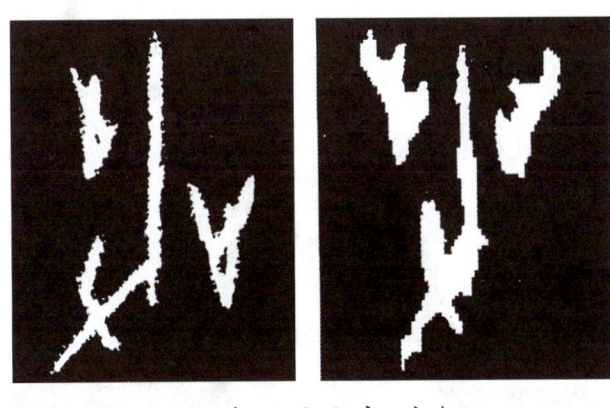

发（甲骨文拓片）

与发组合的词有：发展、发现、发光、发明家、发愤图强等。
Compound words related to the character "发" include:
1. 发展（fā zhǎn）– Development
2. 发现（fā xiàn）– Discovery
3. 发光（fā guāng）– Emit light
4. 发明家（fā míng jiā）– Inventor
5. 发愤图强（fā fèn tú qiáng）– Strive for self-improvement

第十三单元

xíng
行

甲骨文"行"字,像是十字路口形。属象形字。

The character "行" in Oracle Bone Script resembles the shape of a crossroads. It belongs to the category of pictographic characters.

行(示意图)

第十三单元

丿 彳 彳 行 行
1　2　3　4　5　6

楷书书写顺序

本义是指十字路口。可引申为道路、行列、行辈、行业、行走、流通、做、行为、将要、可以等义。

The original meaning refers to a crossroads. It can be extended to mean road, line, generation, profession, walking, circulation, doing, behavior, about to, able to, etc.

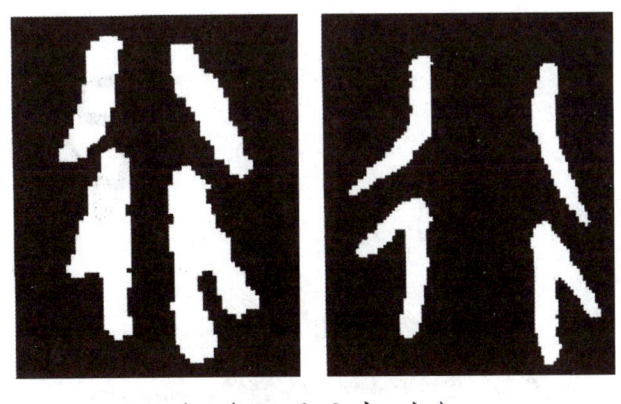

行（甲骨文拓片）

与行组合的词有：行为、行动、行星、行之有效等。

Compound words related to the character "行" include:

1. 行为（xíng wéi）– Behavior
2. 行动（xíng dòng）– Action
3. 行星（xíng xīng）– Planet
4. 行之有效（xíng zhī yǒu xiào）– Effective

第十三单元

zhèng

正

甲骨文"正"字，从口，表示村落或城邑，也表示方向与目标。从止，像脚趾之形，指脚步在向城邑等目标行进。属会意字。

The Oracle Bone Script character "正" consists of two parts: "口"（kǒu）, representing a village or a city, as well as a direction and a goal; and "止"（zhǐ）, resembling the shape of toes, indicating footsteps moving toward the city or goal. It belongs to the category of associative compounds.

正（示意图）

第十三单元

一 丁 下 厊 正
1　2　3　4　5

楷书书写顺序

　　本义是指径直向城邑进发。可引申为正当、端正、正面、合规范、纯正、恰巧、居中、主体等义。

The original meaning is to proceed directly towards a city. It can be extended to signify correctness, upright, front-facing, conformity, purity, coincidence, centrality, and main body.

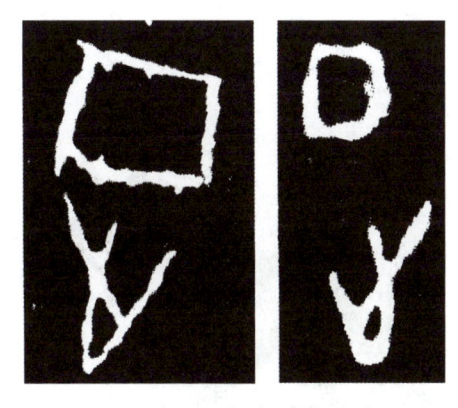

正（甲骨文拓片）

　　与正组合的词有：正面、正确、正常化、正大光明等。
Compound words related to the character "正" include:
1. 正面（zhèng miàn）– Frontal; Front-facing
2. 正确（zhèng què）– Correct; Right
3. 正常化（zhèng cháng huà）– Normalization
4. 正大光明（zhèng dà guāng míng）– Fair and aboveboard

shì

世

甲骨文"世"字，上从竹，像竹木之形，下从止，像人之足趾之形，只是止上部有三点画，并有虚者、有实者，其义无别。此为指事符，表示与"止"的区别，而仍以止为声，甲骨文以笹为世，笹从世声。属形声指事字。

The Oracle Bone Script character "世" depicts a bamboo-like structure on the top and a foot with toes on the bottom. The only difference between the "止" depiction and the shape of toes is that there are just three dot strokes on the top of the "止" depiction. And some of these three dot strokes are virtual, while others are physical. But they have the same meanings. The differentiation between a solid and a hollow representation of the "止" component indicates a distinction but retains the phonetic aspect, with "止" providing the sound. In Oracle Bone Script, "世" was written as "笹", with the character "笹" borrowing its sound. This character belongs to the category of compound-semantic phonetic characters.

世（示意图）

第十四单元

一　十　卅　卋　世
1　2　3　4　5

楷书书写顺序

本义指世代更替延叠。引申为父子世代相继、人的一生、地质年代单位、时代、世界、后嗣、继承等义。

The original meaning refers to the succession and continuity of generations. It can be extended to mean successive generations of fathers and sons, a person's lifetime, geological epochs, eras, the world, descendants, inheritance, and so on.

世（甲骨文拓片）

与世组合的词有：世纪、世俗、世道、世界观、世世代代等。
Compound words related to the character "世" include:
1. 世纪（shì jì）– Century
2. 世俗（shì sú）– Secular; Worldly
3. 世道（shì dào）– Moral principles; Ways of the world
4. 世界观（shì jiè guān）– Worldview; Ideology
5. 世世代代（shì shì dài dài）– For generations; Through generations

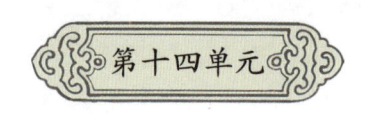

qīn

亲

甲骨文"亲"字，上从宀，俗称宝盖头，像房屋之形，下从新，或从薪，像以斫木之形，这里兼作标声。属形声字。两周金文从见、辛声，表示常见。"親"为繁休字，今汉字简化规范用其声旁亲的省形来表示，写作"亲"为正体。

The Oracle Bone Script character "亲" consists of "宀" on the top, representing a roof, and "新"（xīn）or "薪"（xīn）on the bottom, resembling the action of chopping wood with an axe. This character is a pictophonetic compound. In ancient bronze inscriptions of the Zhou Dynasty, it was written with "见"（jiàn）or "辛"（xīn）, which serve as phonetic components, indicating a common appearance.

"親" is the traditional form, while the simplified form now uses the phonetic component "亲" to represent it.

亲（示意图）

第十四单元

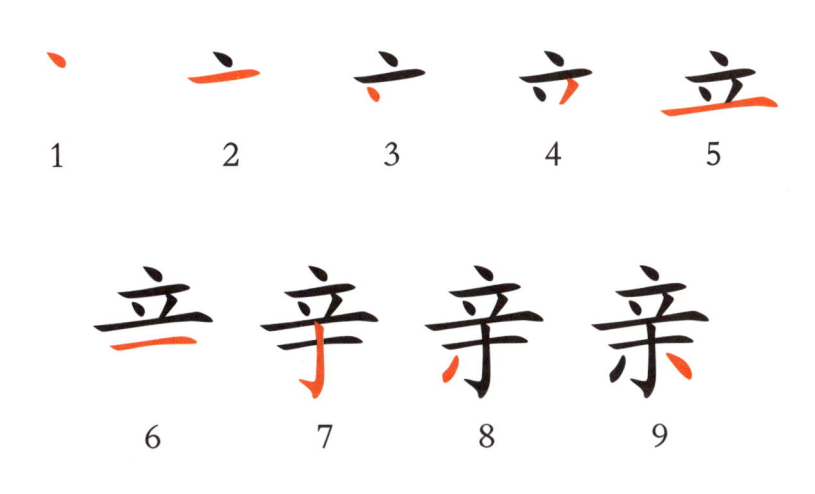

丶 亠 六 亢 立
1　2　3　4　5

立 辛 辛 亲
6　7　8　9

楷书书写顺序

本义为亲近。可引申为父母、新旧、亲属、本身等义。

The original meaning refers to being close or intimate. It can be extended to mean parents, new and old, relatives, oneself, and so on.

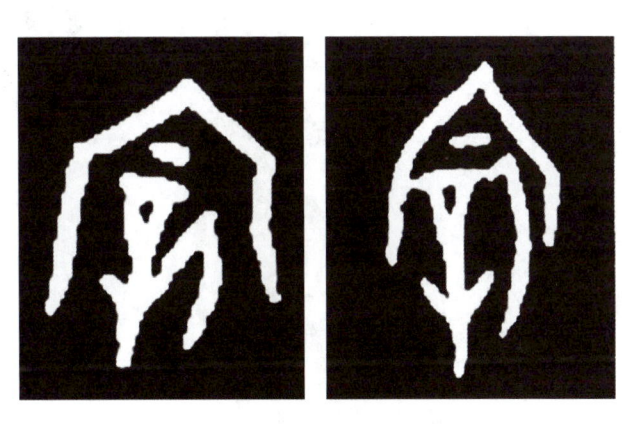

亲（甲骨文拓片）

与亲组合的词有：亲自、亲切、亲友、亲密无间等。
Compound words related to the character "亲" include:

1. 亲自（qīn zì）– Personally
2. 亲切（qīn qiè）– Kind; Cordial
3. 亲友（qīn yǒu）– Relatives and friends
4. 亲密无间（qīn mì wú jiàn）– Intimate and inseparable

第十四单元

rán

然

甲骨文"然"是"燃"的本字,从犬,像狗之形;从火,像燃烧之火堆形。表示以火烧烤犬肉之意。属会意字。"燃"与"然"互相通假。

The Oracle Bone Script character "然" or "燃" depicts a dog and fire, symbolizing the act of roasting dog meat over a fire. It belongs to the category of compound ideogram characters. "燃" and "然" are interchangeable in usage.

然(示意图)

第十四单元

ノ	ク	タ	夕	夕	夘
1	2	3	4	5	6

夕大	犬	狄	然	然	然
7	8	9	10	11	12

楷书书写顺序

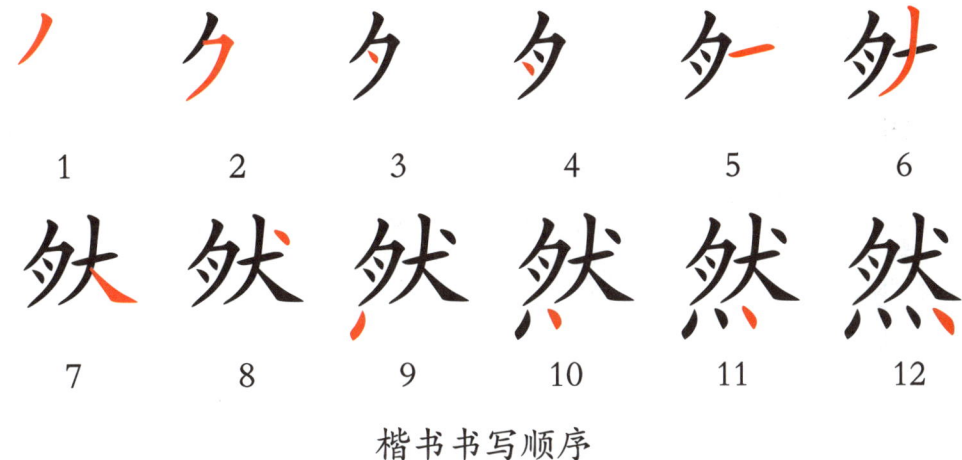

本义为燃烧。可引申为合理的、正确的、样子、这样、然而等义。

The original meaning is burning. It can be extended to mean resonable, correct, appearance, like this, however, and so on.

然（甲骨文拓片）

与然组合的词有：然后、然而、自然美等。

Compound words related to the character "然" include:

1. 然后（rán hòu）– Afterwards
2. 然而（rán ér）– However
3. 自然美（zì rán měi）– Natural beauty

267

第十四单元

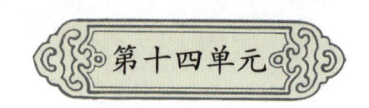

ér

而

甲骨文"而"字,像是颔下所长出的须毛之形。属象形字。

The Oracle Bone Script character "而" resembles the facial hair growing below the chin. It belongs to the category of pictographic characters.

而(示意图)

第十四单元

一 厂 广 丙 而 而
1　2　3　4　5　6

楷书书写顺序

本义是指颔下胡须。可引申为好像、就是、你、才、并列等义。

The original meaning refers to the facial hair growing below the chin. It can also be extended to mean seems like, just is, you, just, paralleling, among other meanings.

而（甲骨文拓片）

与而组合的词有：而且、而是、周而复始、自下而上等。
Compound words related to the character "而" include:
1. 而且（ér qiě）– Moreover
2. 而是（ér shì）– But rather
3. 周而复始（zhōu ér fù shǐ）– Cycle repeatedly
4. 自下而上（zì xià ér shàng）– From bottom to top

shǐ

使

甲骨文"使"是"事"的本字,上方像是狩猎工具猎叉之形,下从"又",像手之形。表示手持捕猎工具去田猎做事之意。属会意字。通假"事""吏"字。

The Oracle Bone Script character "使" or "事" depicts a hunting tool resembling a hunting fork above, with a hand-like shape below. It signifies using a hunting tool to hunt or engage in activities in the fields. This character is a compound ideogram, and it is interchangeable with "事" and "吏".

使(示意图)

第十四单元

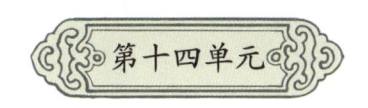

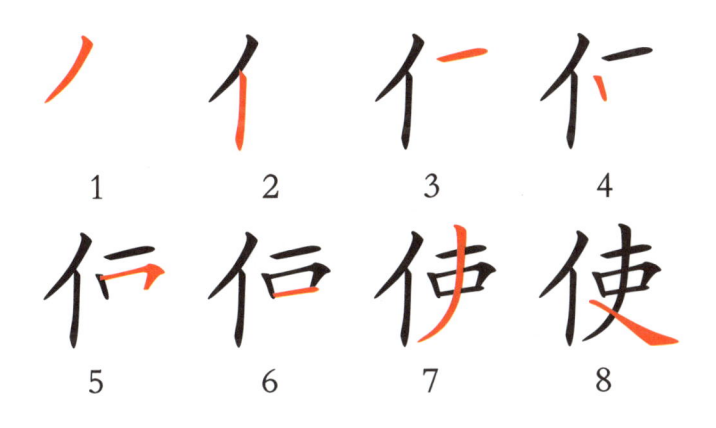

ノ 亻 仁 仁
1　2　3　4

仁 仨 使 使
5　6　7　8

楷书书写顺序

本义指田猎做事。引申为派遣、使用、使唤等义。
The original meaning refers to hunting or engaging in activities in the fields. It can be extended to mean dispatching, using, or letting someone do something.

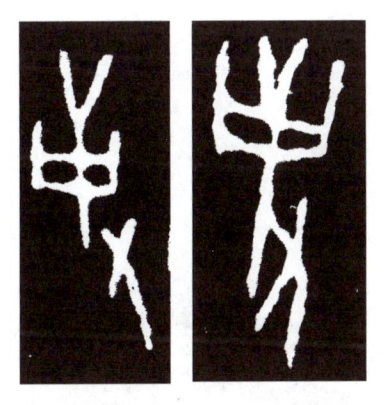

使（甲骨文拓片）

与使组合的词有：使馆、使用、使劲、使命感等。
Compound words related to the character "使" include:
1. 使馆（shǐ guǎn）— Embassy
2. 使用（shǐ yòng）— Use; Utilize
3. 使劲（shǐ jìn）— Exert force; Make an effort
4. 使命感（shǐ mìng gǎn）— Sense of mission

wú

无

甲骨文"无"字即"亡"字,与"臣"字一样像人之侧目,但此"无"字缺了"眼珠",为无眼珠的臣。是"盲"的本字。属象形字。通假"盲""亡"二字。

The Oracle Bone Script character "无" is the same as the character "亡", resembling the profile of a person. This "无" lacks the "eye" component, depicting a minister without eyes, serving as the original character for "盲" (blind). It belongs to the category of pictographic characters. "无" is interchangeable with "盲" and "亡".

无(示意图)

第十四单元

一 二 于 无
1　2　3　4

楷书书写顺序

本义是指无眼珠，目盲，即眼瞎。可引申为没有、无、无辨别力等义。
The original meaning refers to lacking eyeballs, or being blind. It can be extended to mean without, lack of, or unable to discern.

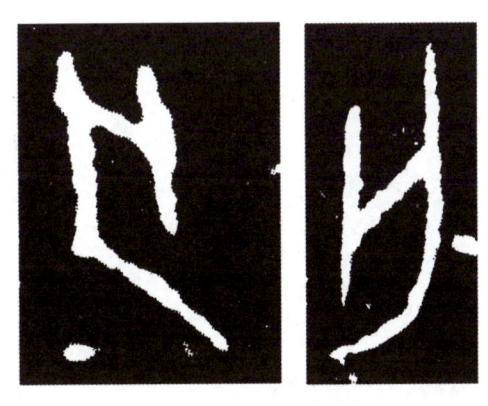

无（甲骨文拓片）

与无组合的词有：无数、无关、无视、无所谓、无所畏惧等。
Compound words related to the character "无" include:
1. 无数（wú shù）– Countless; Numerous
2. 无关（wú guān）– Irrelevant; Unrelated
3. 无视（wú shì）– Disregard; Ignore
4. 无所谓（wú suǒ wèi）– It doesn't matter; Be indifferent
5. 无所畏惧（wú suǒ wèi jù）– Fearless; Dauntless

qí

其

甲骨文"其"字即"箕"字,像是簸箕形,指用竹子编的扬米去糠的农具,前为敞口有舌形,后有半圆之帮可把持。属象形字。

The Oracle Bone Script character "其" is the same as the character "箕", resembling the shape of a winnowing basket, which is a farming tool made of bamboo used to separate rice grains from chaff. It has an open mouth with a tongue-shaped extension in the front and a semi-circular handle in the back for grip. It belongs to the category of pictographic characters.

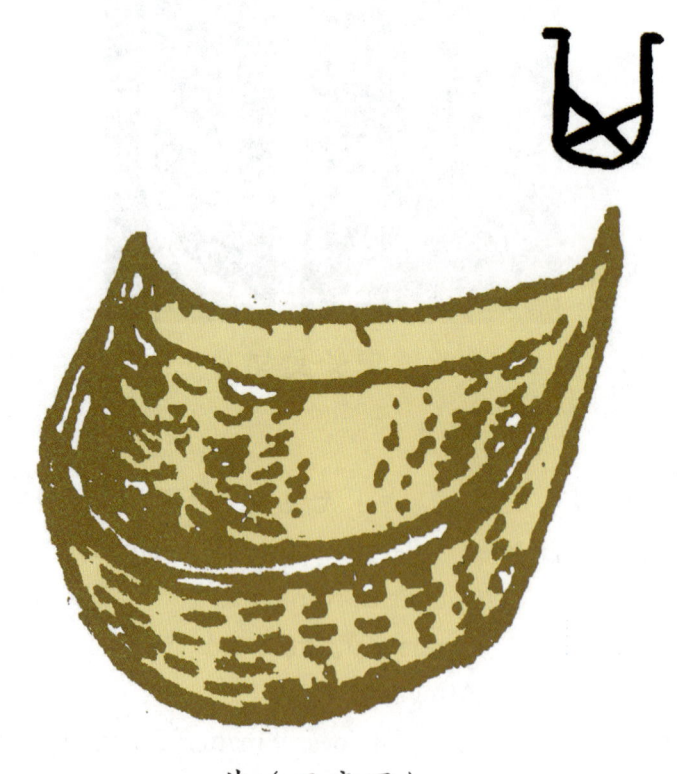

其(示意图)

第十四单元

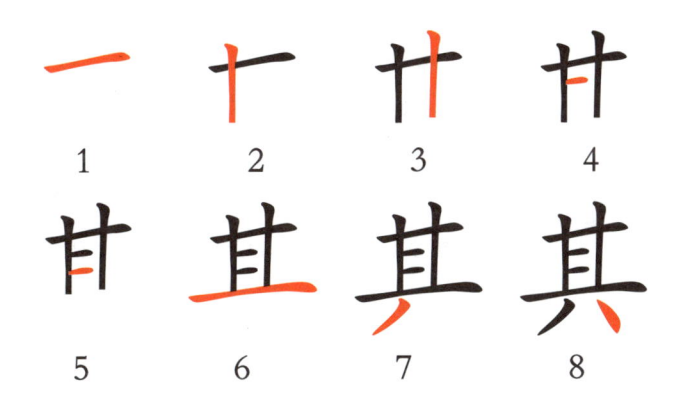

一	十	廾	甘
1	2	3	4

甘	其	其	其
5	6	7	8

楷书书写顺序

本义是指簸箕。可引申为箕形纹器物、自己的、代词、那些、举例等义。

The original meaning refers to a winnowing basket. It can be extended to mean objects shaped like a winnowing basket, self-owned items, pronouns, those, examples, and so on.

其（甲骨文拓片）

与其组合的词有：其他、其实、其余、其乐无穷等。
Compound words related to the character"其"include:
1. 其他（qí tā）– Other
2. 其实（qí shí）– Actually; In fact
3. 其余（qí yú）– The rest; Others
4. 其乐无穷（qí lè wú qióng）– Endless joy; Boundless fun

cǐ
此

甲骨文"此"字,从止,像人的脚趾形;从人,像人之侧视形,后讹为从匕。此可会人之脚趾站立在此处之意。属会意字。通假"跐"字。

The character "此"（cǐ）in Oracle Bone Script consists of "止"（zhǐ）, resembling the shape of a person's toes, and "人"（rén）, resembling the side view of a person, later miswritten as "匕"（bǐ）. This may indicate the idea of a person's toes standing at a particular place. This character belongs to the category of ideographic characters. It is also interchangeable with the character "跐"（cǐ）.

此（示意图）

第十四单元

丨 卜 ㄣ 止 止 此
1　2　3　4　5　6

楷书书写顺序

本义是指站立在此处。可引申为这个、如此、乃、则等义。

The original meaning refers to standing at this place. It can be extended to mean this, thus, then, and so on.

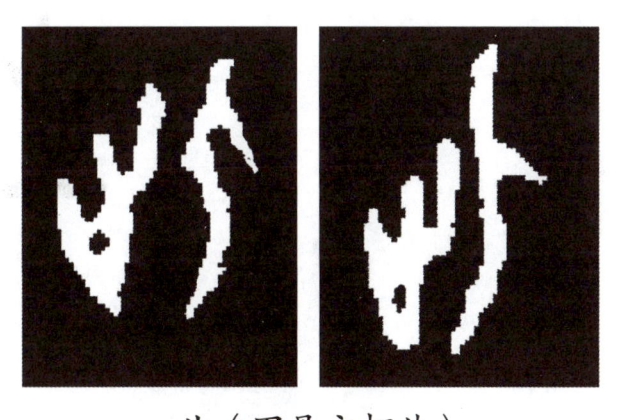

此（甲骨文拓片）

与此组合的词有：此外、此刻、此起彼伏等。

Compound words related to the character "此" include:
1. 此外（cǐ wài）– Besides; In addition
2. 此刻（cǐ kè）– At this moment; Now
3. 此起彼伏（cǐ qǐ bǐ fú）– Happening in succession

第十四单元

zhī
之

甲骨文"之"字,从止,像脚趾形;从一,表示此地是出发的地方,即人足从这里前往。属指事字。

The character "之" in Oracle Bone Script is depicted with a component resembling toes, and another component resembling the Chinese character "一"（number/digit 1）, indicating that it is the starting point. It signifies a person's foot departing from this place. This character belongs to the category of indicative characters.

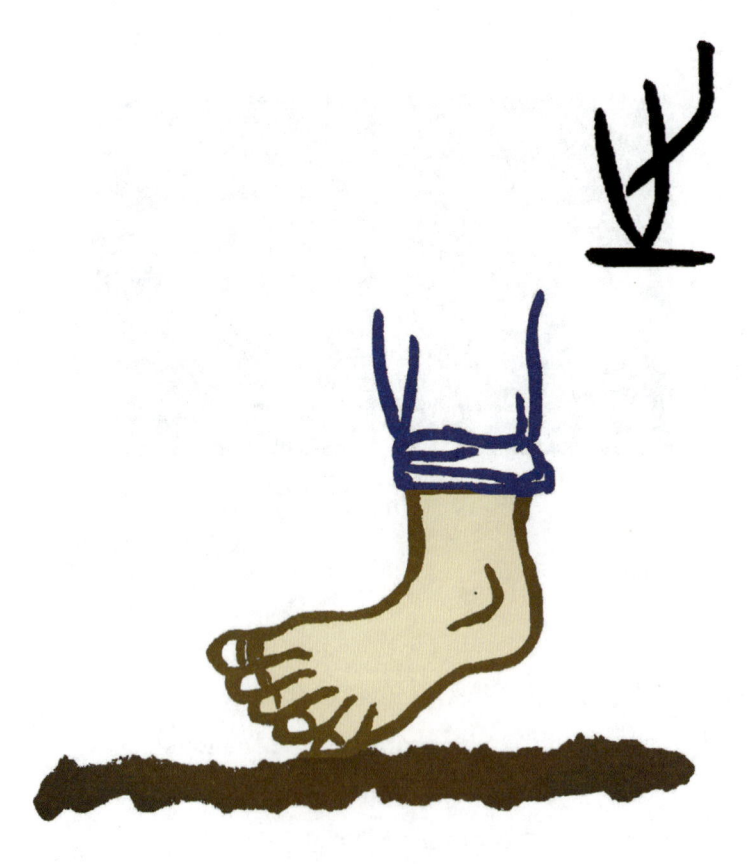

之（示意图）

第十四单元

丶 ㇇ 之
1　2　3

楷书书写顺序

本义是指前往。可引申为到、往、她、他、这、这个、的、符合、舒服等义。
The original meaning is to go or to depart. It can be extended to mean to, towards, her, him, this, this one, of , in accordance with, comfortable, and so on.

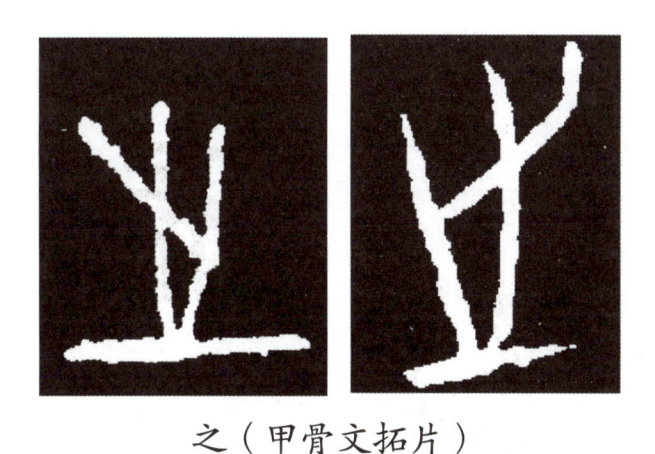

之（甲骨文拓片）

与之组合的词有：之间、之后、之所以、取之不尽等。
Compound words related to the character "之" include:
1. 之间（zhī jiān）– Between
2. 之后（zhī hòu）– After; Later
3. 之所以（zhī suǒ yǐ）– The reason why
4. 取之不尽（qǔ zhī bù jìn）– Endless; Inexhaustible

第十四单元

yú

于

(通"竽")

甲骨文"于"字,左边像一种吹奏性的乐器,当属我国最早的"竽";右边把"于"包套其中,象征着乐声婉转悠扬。属象形字。通假"竽"字。

The Oracle Bone Script character "于" depicts a musical instrument on the left side, resembling the ancient Chinese musical instrument called "yu"(竽). On the right side, "于" is wrapped within it, symbolizing the melodious sound of music. "于" is interchangeable with the character "竽", and is classified as a pictographic character.

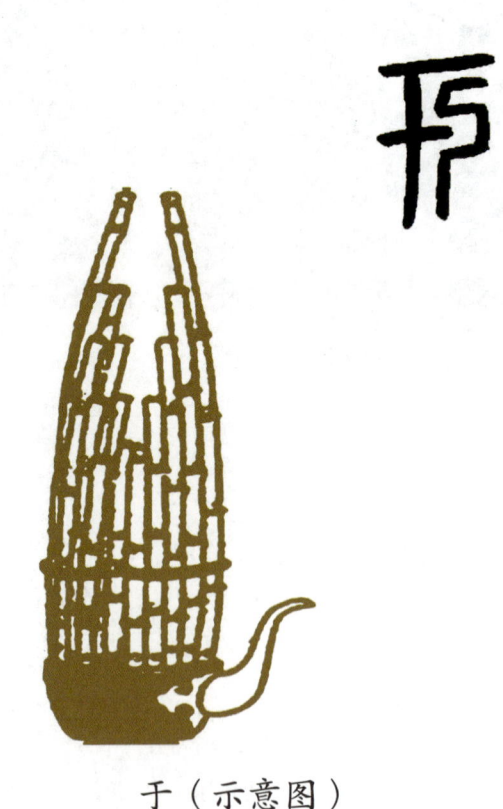

于(示意图)

第十四单元

一　二　于
1　　2　　3

楷书书写顺序

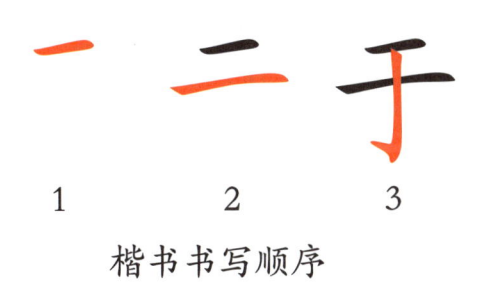

本义是指吹竽时乐音婉转悠扬之状。可引申为迂回曲折、生气舒缓、气损、疑问语气词、在、对、到、用、惊叹、呼告、毁坏等义。

The original meaning refers to the melodious sound produced when playing the "yu" (ancient Chinese musical instrument). It can be extended to imply twists and turns, relaxed atmosphere, weakening of vitality, interrogative modal particles, in, for, to, use, conveying surprise, making announcements, causing damage, and other meanings.

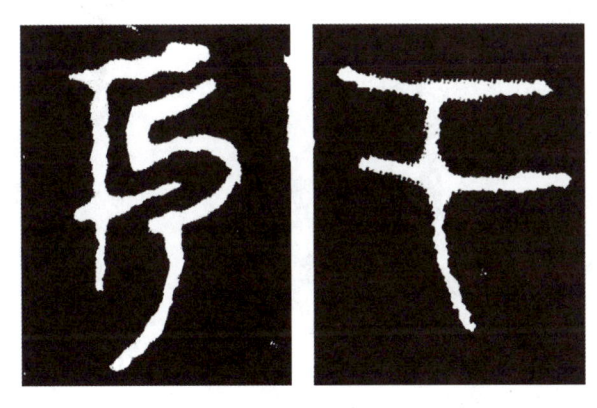

于（甲骨文拓片）

与于组合的词有：于是、于事无补、于心不忍等。
Compound words related to the character "于" include:
1. 于是（yú shì）– Therefore; Thus
2. 于事无补（yú shì wú bǔ）– No use in doing so
3. 于心不忍（yú xīn bù rěn）– Not to have the heart to

第十五单元

xìng

幸

甲骨文"幸"字，像古代的刑具手梏之形。殷墟出土的陶囚俑两手加梏，其梏如字形。两手之腕枷入中孔，绳缚两端，用于拘执俘虏与罪隶。通假"梏"。属象形字。

The Oracle Bone Script character "幸" resembles the ancient handcuffs used as a form of punishment. In the pottery figurines excavated from the Yin ruins, both hands of the prisoners are bound with handcuffs, which resemble the shape of the character. The handcuffs were used to restrain prisoners and slaves by threading the wrist irons through the central hole and tying the ends with ropes. This character belongs to the category of pictographic characters.

幸（示意图）

第十五单元

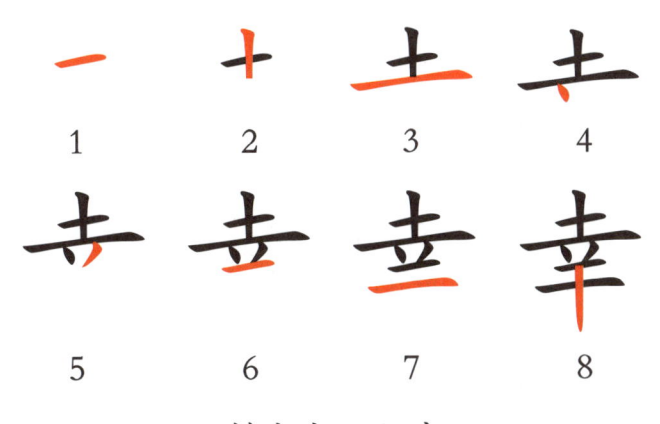

楷书书写顺序

本义是指手梏。今假借作幸福之幸，且可引申为幸福、欢喜、希冀、幸亏、庆幸、驾临等义。

The original meaning refers to handcuffs. In modern usage, it is borrowed to signify happiness or good fortune, and can be extended to mean joy, hope, luckily, fortunate, and arrived.

幸（甲骨文拓片）

与幸组合的词有：幸好、幸存、幸运儿、三生有幸等。
Compound words related to the character "幸" include:

1. 幸好（xìng hǎo）– Fortunately
2. 幸存（xìng cún）– Survive
3. 幸运儿（xìng yùn ér）– Lucky fellow
4. 三生有幸（sān shēng yǒu xìng）– A great honor; A great privilege

fú

福

甲骨文"福"字,从示,像神主牌位或祭祀台。从畐,表示酒器。从手(或省手),像人之两手形。整个字形像是举起手中的酒樽,向神主牌位或祭台倾倒美酒作祭拜之状,累加示旁可会为祭祀神灵以求福佑之意。有带点状者为抛洒溢出的酒液。属会意字。

The character "福" in Oracle Bone Script depicts the image of a sacrificial altar or shrine, represented by the radical "示", combined with a vessel for pouring wine, indicated by the radical "畐". Additionally, there is the component of hands (or a simplified version thereof), resembling the shape of two hands. The character resembles the action of pouring wine from a vessel held in the hands onto the sacrificial altar or shrine, symbolizing the act of offering sacrifices to seek blessings from the gods. The dots added signifies the overflowing or spilling of wine. This character is a compound ideogram.

福(示意图)

第十五单元

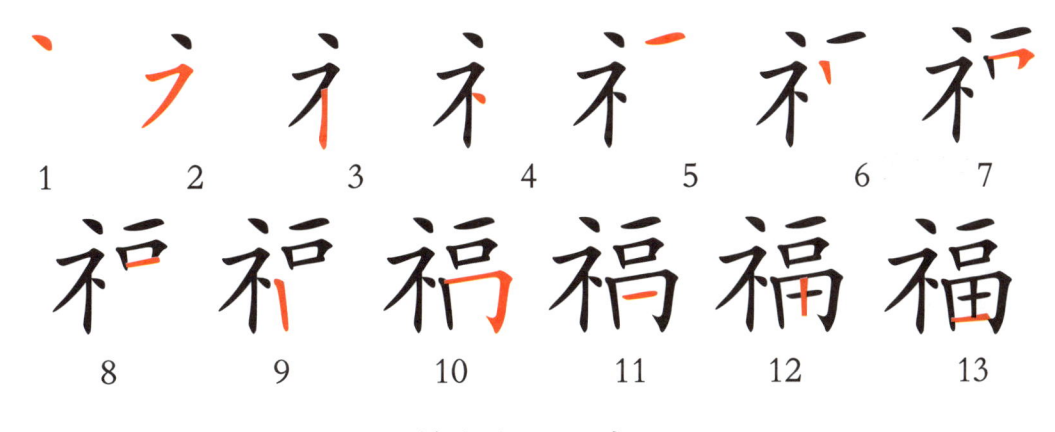

丶	⼀	⼀	⼀	⼀	⼀	⼀
1	2	3	4	5	6	7

礻	礻	福	福	福	福
8	9	10	11	12	13

楷书书写顺序

本义指举酒福佑。可引申为充满、求福、保佑、福气、妇女行礼等义。

The original meaning of "福" is to raise wine for blessings. It can be extended to mean be full of, seeking blessings, blessing, good fortune, and women's ceremonial gestures, among others.

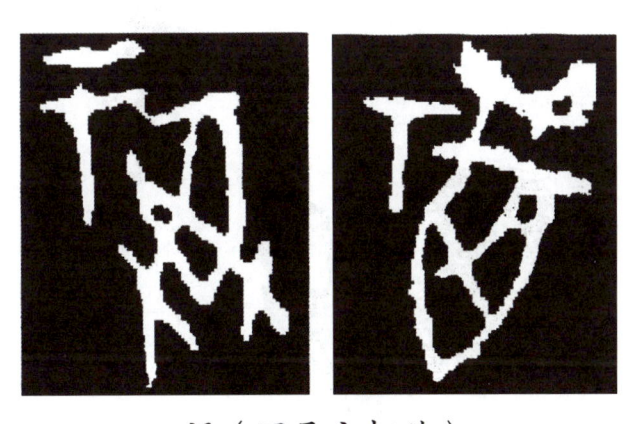

福（甲骨文拓片）

与福组合的词有：福建、福分、福利院、有福同享等。
Compound words related to the character "福" include:
1. 福建（fú jiàn）– Fujian（a province in China）
2. 福分（fú fèn）– Fortunate destiny
3. 福利院（fú lì yuàn）– Welfare institution
4. 有福同享（yǒu fú tóng xiǎng）– Share blessings together

wàng

望

甲骨文"望"字，从臣（代表竖目）、从人、从土，像人登高举目瞭望之形。其"壬"代表朝廷，又意指臣朝君之意。殷、西周时加了月符，臣改亡声，以示人站在土堆高处望月。属会意字。

The Oracle Bone Script character "望" consists of the components "臣"（representing upright eyes）, "人"（person）, and "土"（earth）, resembling a person standing high and looking into the distance. "壬" represents the court, implying the minister looking up to the ruler. During the Yin and Western Zhou dynasties, a moon symbol was added, and the pronunciation shifted to signify a person standing on a mound of earth and looking at the moon. This character is a compound ideogram.

望（示意图）

第十五单元

楷书书写顺序

本义指瞭望、望月之意。引申为探望、接近、盼望、景仰、声望等义。

Its original meaning refers to looking into the distance or looking at the moon. It can be extended to mean visiting, approaching, hoping for, admiring, or reputation and prestige.

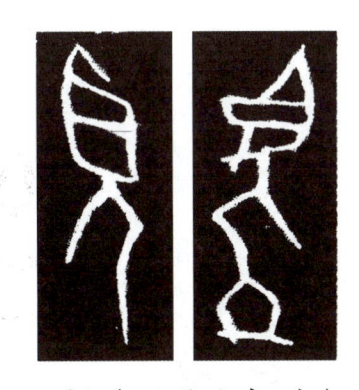

望（甲骨文拓片）

与望组合的词有：望远镜、望尘莫及、望洋兴叹、望梅止渴等。
Compound words related to the character "望" include:

1. 望远镜（wàng yuǎn jìng）– Telescope

2. 望尘莫及（wàng chén mò jí）– Unable to catch up with the dust（figuratively means being left far behind）

3. 望洋兴叹（wàng yáng xīng tàn）– Sigh with emotion when looking out over the sea（figuratively means feeling helpless when facing great challenges）

4. 望梅止渴（wàng méi zhǐ kě）– Quench one's thirst by thinking of plums（figuratively means finding comfort or satisfaction through anticipation）

第十五单元

yóu

由

甲骨文"由"字，从口，像器皿之口形，此口形一般大于其他器物。上从一小圆圈，表示一颗液滴。可会向器皿内注油液之意。属象形字。

The character "由" in Oracle Bone Script consists of "口", resembling the mouth of a vessel, which is generally larger than other objects. Above it, there is a small circle representing a droplet of liquid, indicating the pouring of oil or liquid into the vessel. This character belongs to the category of pictographic characters.

由（示意图）

第十五单元

丨 冂 日 由 由
1　2　3　4　5

楷书书写顺序

本义指油液滴入器皿内。可引申为凭借、原因、因为、经由、遵从、听凭、自、从等义。

The original meaning refers to the dripping of oil or liquid into a container. It can be extended to mean relying on, reason, because, through, following, letting, from, via, etc.

由（甲骨文拓片）

与由组合的词有：由于、由来、由此可见、由下而上、由浅入深等。
Compound words related to the character "由" include:

1. 由于（yóu yú）– Due to
2. 由来（yóu lái）– Origin; Source
3. 由此可见（yóu cǐ kě jiàn）– It can be seen from this; Hence
4. 由下而上（yóu xià ér shàng）– From bottom to top
5. 由浅入深（yóu qiǎn rù shēn）– From shallow to deep

第十五单元

ān

安

甲骨文"安"字,像一女子两手在腹前交叉,安静地跪坐在屋中之状,以表示平安无事、闲雅安适之意。属会意字。

The Oracle Bone Script character "安" depicts a woman sitting quietly with her hands crossed over her abdomen, suggesting a state of peace and tranquility, as if she were peacefully kneeling in a room. This conveys the meaning of safety, peace, and comfort. This character belongs to the category of associative compound characters.

安(示意图)

第十五单元

丶 丷 宀 宊 宊 安
1　2　3　4　5　6

楷书书写顺序

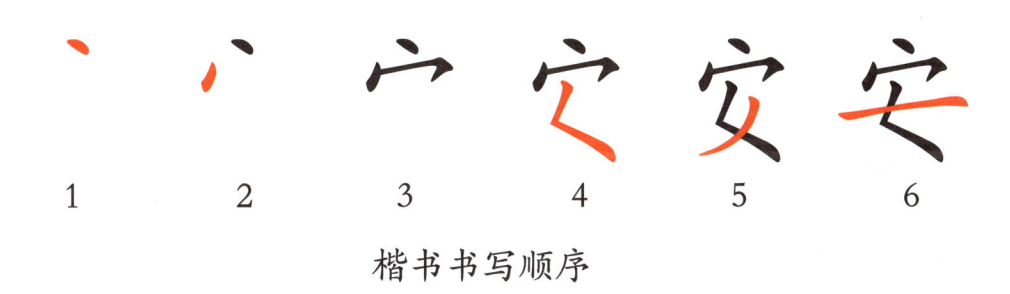

本义是指安静。可引申为安定、安置、舒缓、平安、安详、安然等义。
The original meaning refers to quietness or tranquility. It can be extended to mean stability, placement, relaxation, peace, serenity, and calmness.

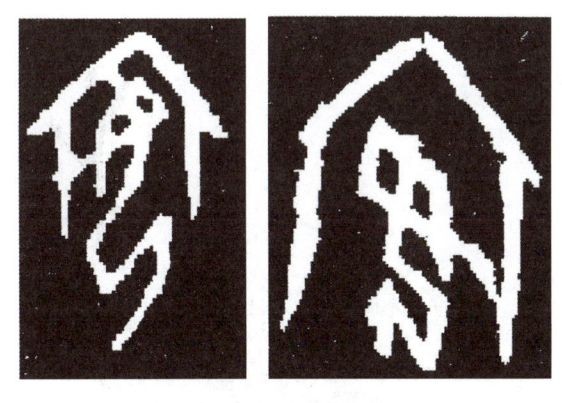

安（甲骨文拓片）

与安组合的词有：安排、安装、安心、安慰、安然无恙等。
Compound words related to the character "安" include:
1. 安排（ān pái）– Arrange
2. 安装（ān zhuāng）– Install
3. 安心（ān xīn）– Feel at ease; Be relieved
4. 安慰（ān wèi）– Comfort; Console
5. 安然无恙（ān rán wú yàng）– Safe and sound; Without mishap

第十五单元

mù
木

甲骨文"木"字，属象形字。像有枝叶、茎秆和根的树木形。属象形字。

The character "木" in Oracle Bone Script is a pictograph, depicting the shape of a tree with branches, leaves, stems, and roots.

木（示意图）

第十五单元

一 十 才 木
1　2　3　4

楷书书写顺序

本义指树木。引申为木头、木器、木料、八音之一、五行之一、质朴、呆笨、星名、麻木等义。

Its original meaning refers to the tree or wood. It can be extended to mean wood, wooden objects, timber, one of the Eight Sounds (in ancient Chinese music theory), one of the Five Elements, simple and plain, stupid, name of a star, numbness, and so on.

木（甲骨文拓片）

与木组合的词有：木板、木偶、木匠、木盆等。
Compound words related to the character "木" include:
1. 木板（mù bǎn）– Wooden board
2. 木偶（mù ǒu）– Puppet
3. 木匠（mù jiàng）– Carpenter
4. 木盆（mù pén）– Wooden basin

第十五单元

shuǐ

水

甲骨文"水"字，曲曲弯弯，外侧虚线表示堤岸，或溅起之水滴；中间实线表示流水，像水流之状。属象形字。

The character "水" （shuǐ） in Oracle Bone Script means "water". It is an ideogram depicting flowing water with curves and lines. The full line in the middle represents the movement of water, while the dashed lines on both sides indicate riverbanks or splashing water droplets.

水（示意图）

第十五单元

亅 汀 氺 水
1　2　3　4

楷书书写顺序

本义作水流。引申为江、河、湖、洋、水之液态、液体物、星名等义。

The original meaning refers to the flow of water. It is extended to mean rivers, lakes, seas, oceans, the liquid water, liquid substances, and names of stars.

水（甲骨文拓片）

与水组合的词有：水平、水果、水稻、水源、水晶、水电站等。

Compound words related to the character "水" include:

1. 水平（shuǐ píng）— Level; Horizontal
2. 水果（shuǐ guǒ）— Fruit
3. 水稻（shuǐ dào）— Rice
4. 水源（shuǐ yuán）— Water source
5. 水晶（shuǐ jīng）— Crystal
6. 水电站（shuǐ diàn zhàn）— Hydroelectric power station

第十五单元

huǒ

火

甲骨文"火"字,像火焰升腾之状,带点者表示烟屑与火苗。属象形字。

The Oracle Bone Script character "火"(huǒ) is a pictogram representing flames rising upwards, often with dots indicating soot and sparks.

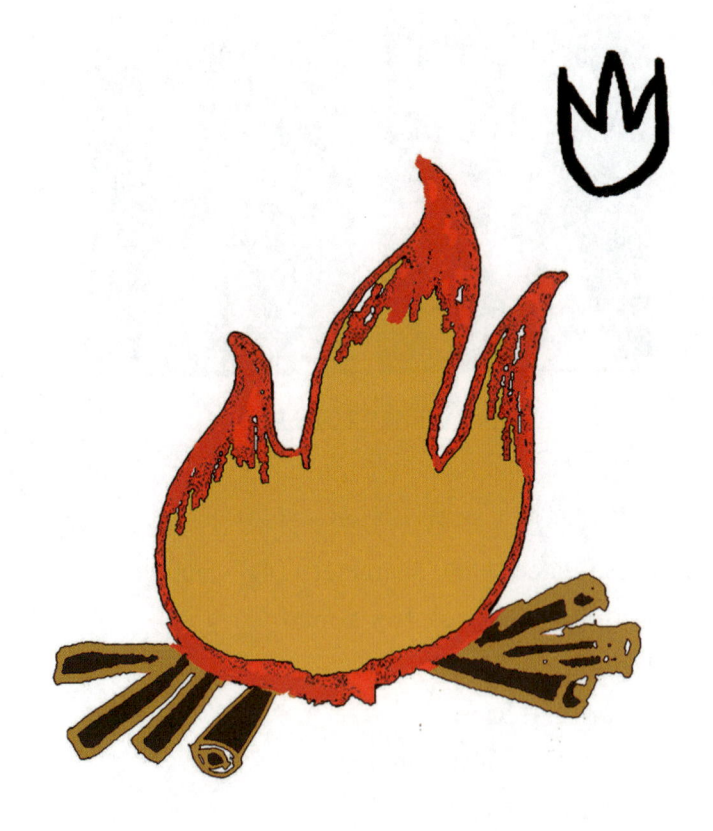

火(示意图)

第十五单元

丶 丷 火 火
1　2　3　4

楷书书写顺序

本义是物体燃烧所形成的火团、火光和烟热。引申为燃烧、发光物、弹药、战争、红色、紧急、脾气暴躁、五行之一等义。

The original meaning refers to the fiery glow and heat produced by the combustion of objects. It can be extended to mean burning, luminous objects, ammunition, warfare, the color red, urgency, fiery temperament, and one of the Five Elements.

火（甲骨文拓片）

与火组合的词有：火车、火箭、火山、火眼金睛等。
Compound words related to the character "火" include:
1. 火车（huǒ chē）– Train
2. 火箭（huǒ jiàn）– Rocket
3. 火山（huǒ shān）– Volcano
4. 火眼金睛（huǒ yǎn jīn jīng）– Sharpened eyesight

第十五单元

yīn

阴

甲骨文"阴"字,从隹,像鸟的侧视形;从亼,本为器物的盖子形,此作标声。表示天气不晴,卜文作天象气候专用字。属形声会意字。

The Oracle Bone Script character "阴" consists of the component "隹", resembling the profile of a bird, and "亼", originally representing the shape of a lid of an object and functioning as a phonetic hint. It indicates a cloudy sky. In Oracle Bone Inscriptions, it was used as a specialized character for weather phenomena and climate. This character is a compound ideogram.

阴(示意图)

第十五单元

了 阝 阝 阴 阴 阴
1　2　3　4　5　6

楷书书写顺序

本义为天气阴。引申为凹进的、背光处、死后的、隐秘、背后、生殖器、带负电的等义。

The original meaning refers to overcast weather. It can be extended to refer to things that are concave or recessed, areas in shadow or behind something, matters pertaining to the deceased, secrecy, the posterior, reproductive organs, or objects carrying a negative charge.

阴（甲骨文拓片）

与阴组合的词有：阴影、阴雨、阴沉沉、阴谋诡计等。
Compound words related to the character "阴" include:
1. 阴影（yīn yǐng）– Shadow
2. 阴雨（yīn yǔ）– Overcast and rainy
3. 阴沉沉（yīn chén chén）– Gloomy
4 阴谋诡计（yīn móu guǐ jì）– Conspiracy and trickery

第十五单元

yáng
阳

甲骨文"阳"字，从昜，从阜。昜之上从日，表示太阳升到了祭神的石阜上方，可会太阳在山南面照耀着祭台之意，与山北面之阴相对。属会意字。"陽"为繁体字。今汉字简化规范写作"阳"为正体。

The Oracle Bone Script character "阳" is a compound ideogram. It consists of "昜" and "阜". "昜" depicts the sun rising above a stone mound used for worship, suggesting the sunlight shining down on the sacrificial altar from the southern side of the mountain, contrasting with the shade on the northern side. In traditional Chinese, it is written as "陽". In modern simplified Chinese, "阳" is the standard form.

阳（示意图）

第十五单元

了 阝 阳 阳 阳 阳
1　2　3　4　5　6

楷书书写顺序

本义是山南之阳。可引申为温暖、鲜明、外露、突起的东西、物体的正面、假装等义。

The original meaning refers to the sun shining on the south side of the mountain. It can be extended to mean warmth, brightness, exposure, prominence of something, the front of an object, and pretending.

阳（甲骨文拓片）

与阳组合的词有：阳光、阳台、阳刚之气等。
Compound words related to the character"阳"include:
1. 阳光（yáng guāng）- Sunshine
2. 阳台（yáng tái）- Balcony
3. 阳刚之气（yáng gāng zhī qì）- Masculine energy

301

后　记

　　2023年7月，英国皇家学会工艺院蔡虹冰院士在中国南京期间，与王本兴、蒋文杰、宋慎之三位商讨：在海外汉语教学中，如何让入选《世界记忆名录》的甲骨文进一步得到应用推广与学习？他们一致认为：因为有了甲骨文才有了今天的汉字，海外学子如果从甲骨文走向汉语世界，是增强学习记忆、丰富学习内容的最佳途径。于是便诞生了《从甲骨文走向汉语世界：150个常见汉字中英文双语对照本》一书。实际上，甲骨文特别具有象形性，其形、音、义易懂、易记、易学，基于这点，通过海外实践教学总结及数据分析，筛选出的高频率150个常见汉字，两相对比，相辅相成，更有意义。我们可从这150个甲骨文字开始，快速阅读和书写，有效地走进汉语世界。此书有几点务请注意：

　　一、每个甲骨文字有汉语读音，有的汉字多音多义，仅以本书所标注的音义为准。

　　二、每个甲骨文字有很多种写法，本书例举一种主要常见常用的写法，其余则可忽略不计。

　　三、每个甲骨文字选有两个甲骨文字原始拓片，此拓片皆为殷墟甲骨原迹。

　　四、每个甲骨文字都配有识字的示意图，从文可知图，从图可知文义。

　　五、甲骨文字所对应的汉字是简体字，皆按楷书汉字书写笔顺写出。

　　六、甲骨文字的字性、出处、本义、引申义皆出自王本兴专著《甲骨文字典》与《甲骨文读本》。

　　七、每个汉字的组词选取三至六个，皆为常见常用，仅供参考。

　　八、本书图文并茂，以清晰、简明扼要为旨，非常适合阅读学习。

编辑、出版一本适合海外读者学习中文汉语的书,是很不容易的,英国皇家学会工艺院蔡虹冰院士提供了第一手教学资料,然后,予与蒋文杰、宋慎之两位先生,从英国到中国通过电子信息多次往返商榷,反复研究,把最好的内容以最好的模式奉献给读者;福建教育出版社为优先、优质出版面世,亦作出了艰辛的努力,于此表示谢忱。

王本兴
甲辰春于中国南京鼓楼区凤凰西街59号四喜堂

Afterword

In July 2023, during her visit to Nanjing, China, Mrs. Cai Hongbing, Fellow of the Royal Society of Arts from the United Kingdom discussed with Mr. Wang Benxing, Mr. Jiang Wenjie, and Mr. Song Shenzhi about how to further promote and utilize Oracle Bone Inscriptions, which have been selected for the "Memory of the World Register," in overseas Chinese language teaching. They unanimously agreed that as the origin of Chinese characters, Oracle Bone Inscriptions play a crucial role in enhancing memory and enriching the learning content for Chinese language learners abroad as they enter the world of Chinese language through Oracle Bone Inscriptions. Hence, the idea for this book,"From Oracle Bone Inscriptions to the World of Chinese Language: A Chinese-English Bilingual Edition of 150 Commonly Used Characters," was born.

In fact, Oracle Bone Inscriptions are particularly iconic, with their forms, sounds, and meanings being easy to understand, remember, and learn. Based on this, through overseas practical teaching experience and data analysis, a set of "high-frequency" 150 commonly used Chinese characters were selected. The comparison and complementarity between the two serve a meaningful purpose. We can start our journey into the world of Chinese language by quickly reading and writing these 150 oracle bone characters.

Here are a few points to note about this book:

1. Each oracle bone character has its Chinese pronunciation, and some Chinese characters have multiple pronunciations and meanings. Only those indicated in this book should be considered.

2. Each oracle bone character has many variations in writing. This book lists one common and frequently used form, while the rest can be ignored.

3. Two original oracle bone rubbings are provided for each character, all of which are from the original Oracle Bone Inscriptions of the Yin Ruins.

4. Each oracle bone character is accompanied by an illustrative diagram, aiding understanding of the character from the text and vice versa.

5. The Chinese characters corresponding to the oracle bone characters are in simplified Chinese characters and are written in regular script stroke order.

6. The character nature, origin, original meaning, and extended meanings of the oracle bone characters are all derived from the works of Wang Benxing, "Dictionary of Oracle Bone Characters," and "Reader of Oracle Bone Inscriptions."

7. Three to six compound words are selected for each character, all of which are common and frequently used, provided for reference only.

8. This book is illustrated and concise, aiming for clarity and brevity, making it very suitable for reading and learning.

Publishing a book suitable for overseas readers to learn Chinese language is not an easy task. Mrs. Cai Hongbing, Fellow of the Royal Society of Arts from the United Kingdom, provided first-hand teaching materials. Then with Mr. Jiang Wenjie and Mr. Song Shenzhi, we exchanged ideas through multiple electronic communications between the United Kingdom and China, conducted repeated research, and dedicated the best content and format to the readers. Fujian Education Press has also made strenuous efforts to prioritize and produce high-quality publications. We express our heartfelt thanks for their contributions.

Wang Benxing
Sixi House, 59 Fenghuang West Street, Gulou District, Nanjing, China
Spring of 2024